D

. a returned on or before

WITHDRAWN

11 3050

051832

THE HENLEY COLLEGE LIBRARY

THE BEST OF

BUSINESS CARD DESIGN 8

SIBLEY/PETEET DESIGN | AUSTIN

ROCKPORT PUBLISHERS

BEVERLY MASSACHUSETTS

First published in the United States of America by Rockport Publishers, a member of Quayside Publishing Group
100 Cummings Center Suite 406-L Beverly, MA 01915-6101 Telephone: (978)282.9590 Fax: (978)283.2742 www.rockpub.com

© 2008 by Rockport Publishers, Inc.

All rights reserved. No part of this book may be reproduced in any form without written permission of the copyright owners. All images in this book have been reproduced with the knowledge and prior consent of the artists concerned, and no responsibility is accepted by producer, publisher, or printer for any infringement of copyright or otherwise, arising from the contents of this publication. Every effort has been made to ensure that credits accurately comply with information supplied. We apologize for any inaccuracies that may have occurred and will resolve inaccurate or missing information in a subsequent reprinting of the book.

Design: Sibley/Peteet Design, Austin | Cover: Rex Peteet | Photography: Ned Witrogen | Hand Photography: Matthew Wetzler | Printed in China

Library of Congress Cataloging-in-Publication Data available | ISBN-13: 978-1-59253-403-6 | ISBN-10: 1-59253-403-1 | 10 9 8 7 6 5 4 3 2 1

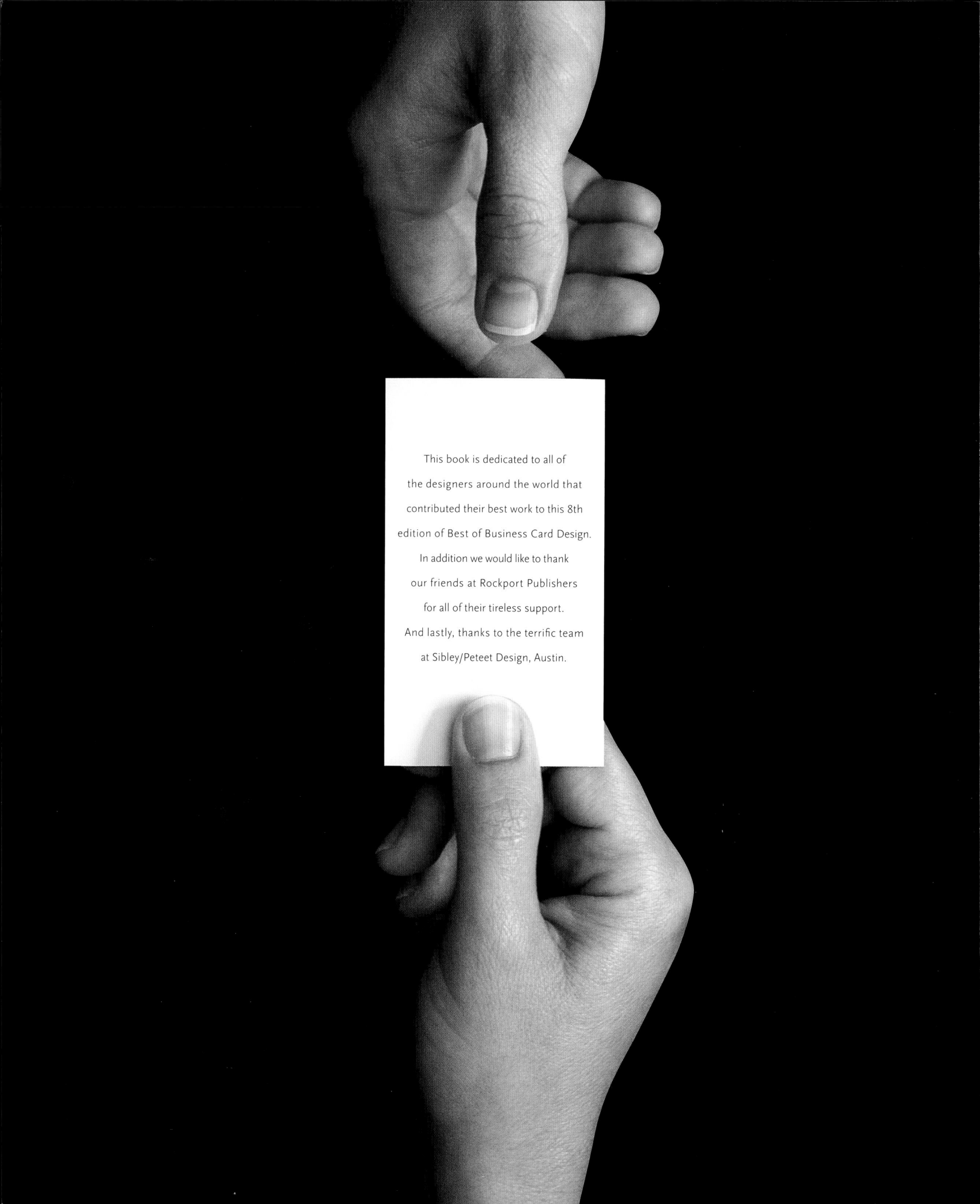

This book is dedicated to all of
the designers around the world that
contributed their best work to this 8th
edition of Best of Business Card Design.
In addition we would like to thank
our friends at Rockport Publishers
for all of their tireless support.
And lastly, thanks to the terrific team
at Sibley/Peteet Design, Austin.

THE BEST OF BUSINESS CARD DESIGN

Business cards have come a long way since their predecessors first appeared in European society in the mid-1600s. These early cards, then referred to as "Visite de Biletes," or visiting cards, eventually evolved into two categories serving distinct purposes: a card used when calling on an individual or group socially, and a card that served as a small advertisement for one's trade or service. Along with their aesthetic and functional evolution, a specific protocol emerged of when and how to use the cards, format standards, proper printing and paper choice, maps (there were no street numbers, so maps were necessary), even intent or purpose. For example, there was an entire vocabulary based on calling card folding. A card folded in half meant the owner was calling on the entire family. A card's upper right corner folded down meant it was delivered personally.

These cards, and their ritual and use, found their way to America in the 1800s. These almost concurrent genres ultimately morphed into what we know today as the business card, and its use has become interchangeable whether calling socially or for business purposes. Thus a whole new category in branding one's self or business was born.

Functionally speaking, the business card has become so much more than an introduction or a method to hype your wares. Business cards tell a story; they open doors; they make a statement; they answer questions; they connect; they unlock and initiate conversation; they provide information and serve as an extension of one's self. Hence–and adverse to what you would expect in this digital age–the very low-tech business card proliferates and maintains a critical purpose in bringing people and business together around the world.

As depicted on the cover of *Best of Business Card Design 8*, we suggest metaphorically many of the things that good business cards do well. This is the criteria we used as a baseline to select the cards that were most successful at telling their individual stories, their degree of appropriateness for a particular business or individual, as well as how uniquely they distinguished themselves. As we juried, we asked ourselves: Does the card appropriately and efficiently communicate? Is the information easily accessible? Is it innovative in the genre? Overdone? Is it practical? (We gave wide berth here, and measured by the necessity to concept, and allowed real creativity to trump mass production feasibility.) Or did we just think it was cool, and wish we had done it?

After reviewing thousands of entries from more than 25 countries, we selected close to 400 of the very best. We saw a lot of laser die cuts, cards with silkscreen on Plexiglas, applied stickers that wrap, embossing, sewing, folding, punching, foiling, and elaborate printing on both sides. By contrast, we also saw the very restrained and elegant. Here you will discover extraordinary examples of each. We hope you are inspired by this eighth edition, giving you another bi-annual snapshot of how the world is connecting itself, and a closer look at how far the visiting card has come since that first introduction more than 350 years ago.

1

Monica Starr • AIFD
eighteen FLOWERS • Kansas City, MO
816.421.1717 • www.18flowers.com

eighteen
FLOWERS

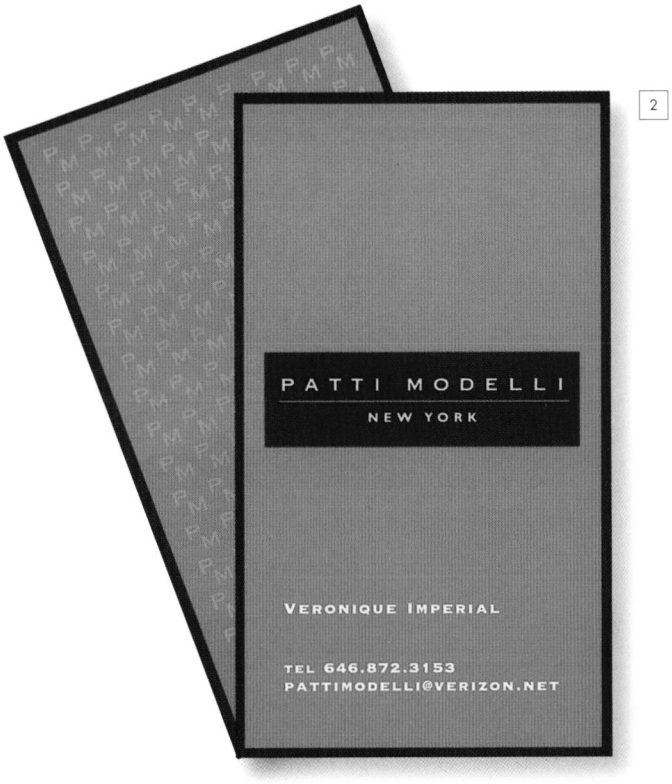

2

3

1

design firm: Bungalow Creative
art director: Christopher Huelshorst
designer: Carrie Kish
client: Eighteen Flowers
software/hardware: Quark Xpress
paper/materials: Fox River Star White 110 lb cover

2

design firm: Wing Chan Design, Inc.
art director: Wing Chan
designer: Wing Chan
client: Patti Modelli
software/hardware: Quark Xpress
paper/materials: Sappi Opus 120 lb gloss cover

3

design firm: Nocturnal Graphic Design Studio
art director: Ken Peters
designer: Ken Peters
illustrator: Nocturnal Graphic Design Studios

1

BARRON LAU
CEO | CREATIVE DIRECTOR

E-MAIL: BARRONL@PRESSURE.ORG
BLACKBERRY PIN: 30075CCE
MOBILE: 416-805-8002
IM: BARRONL@PRESSURE.ORG

2820 14TH AVE., SUITE 101
MARKHAM, ONTARIO
L3R 0S9
PHONE: 905-305-0979 x11
FAX: 905-305-0415
WWW.PRESSURE.ORG

2

3

1

design firm: Pressure
art director: Jun Woo
designer: Vasilios Goulopoulos
client: Pressure
software/hardware: Adobe Illustrator CS2
paper/materials: 12 pt cardstock/custom label

2

design firm: Design Ranch
art director: Michelle Sonderegger and Igred Sidie
designer: Tad Carpenter and Rachel Karaca
client: Nara
software/hardware: Adobe Illustrator and Photoshop

3

design firm: W Design
art director: Kristy Weyhrich
designer: Kristy Weyhrich
client: W Design
software/hardware: Adobe Illustrator and Quark Xpress
paper/materials: Classic Crest, 2 PMS

FRENCH LEAVE

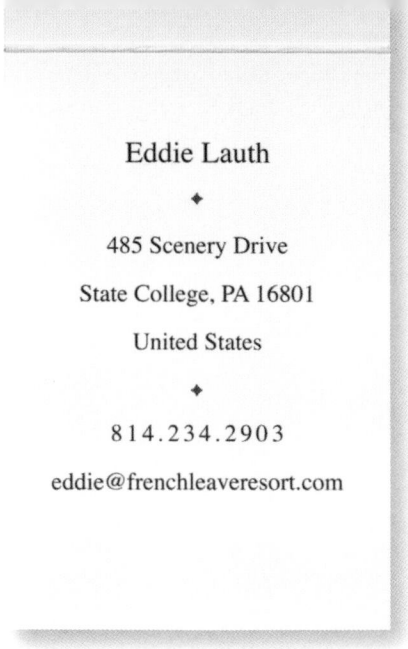
Eddie Lauth
485 Scenery Drive
State College, PA 16801
United States
814.234.2903
eddie@frenchleaveresort.com

1

Mindd Foundation
PO Box 151 Vaucluse
NSW 2030 Australia
T +61 2 9388 7383
www.mindd.org
info@mindd.org
Leslie Embersits
Metabolic
Immuno
Neurological
Digestive
Disorders

Mindd
Foundation

Mindd Foundation
PO Box 151 Vaucluse
NSW 2030 Australia
T +61 2 9388 7383
www.mindd.org
info@mindd.org
Metabolic
Immuno
Neurological
Digestive
Disorders

2

3

ASFOOR & KHATIB TRADING GROUP

P.O.Box: 22733 Safat 13088 Kuwait
Tel.: (+965) 57 47 374 - Fax: (+965) 57 18 476
www.aktgroup.net - tkhatib@aktgroup.net

TAREK KHATIB
DEPUTY MANAGING DIRECTOR

4

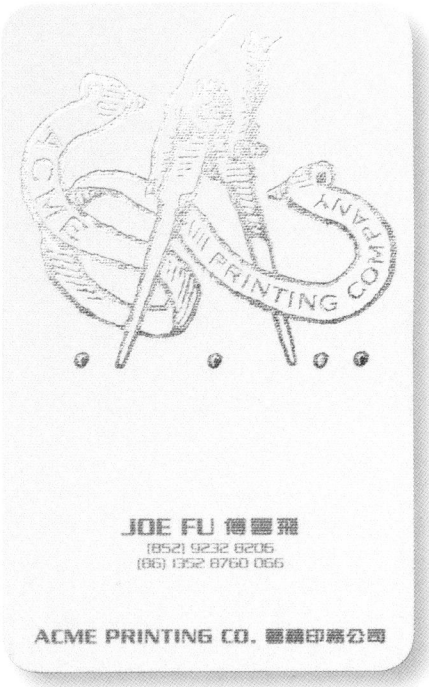

1

design firm: Sommese Design
art director: Kristin Sommese and Lanny Sommese
designer: Kristin Sommese, Lanny Sommese, and Ryan Russell
client: Lauth Development Co.
paper/materials: Beckett Expression Radiance

2

design firm: There
art director: There
designer: There
client: Mindd Foundation
software/hardware: Adobe Illustrator
paper/materials: Various

3

design firm: Paragon Marketing Communications
art director: Louai Alasfahani
designer: Khalid Al-Rifae
client: Asfoor & Khatib Trading Group
software/hardware: Adobe Illustrator
paper/materials: Cache 350 gsm with lamination

4

design firm: Root Idea
art director: Ken Lee
designer: Ken Lee
illustrator: Ken Lee
client: Acme Printing
software/hardware: Photoshop and Adobe Illustrator
paper/materials: Antalis, Reaction Alpine Sparkling Water

Washington, D.C.
202.337.4112
Las Vegas, Nevada
702.364.5888
abalv.com

ABA
Todd-Avery Lenahan
PRINCIPAL & CEO

1

LOUVIERE + VANESSA
Jeff Louviere + Vanessa S. Brown
732 Mazant Street | New Orleans, Louisiana 70117
louviereandvanessa.com
504-940-5498

2

3

1

design firm: SK+G Advertising
art director: Steve Averitt
designer: Steve Averitt
client: Avery Brooks + Associates Design
software/hardware: Adobe InDesign
paper/materials: Fox River Sundance Felt Warm White 100 lb cover, pearlescent foil and letterpressing

2

design firm: Louviere + Vanessa
art director: Jeff Louviere
designer: Jeff Louviere
client: Louviere + Vanessa
software/hardware: Adobe InDesign and Photoshop
paper/materials: 4 color offset

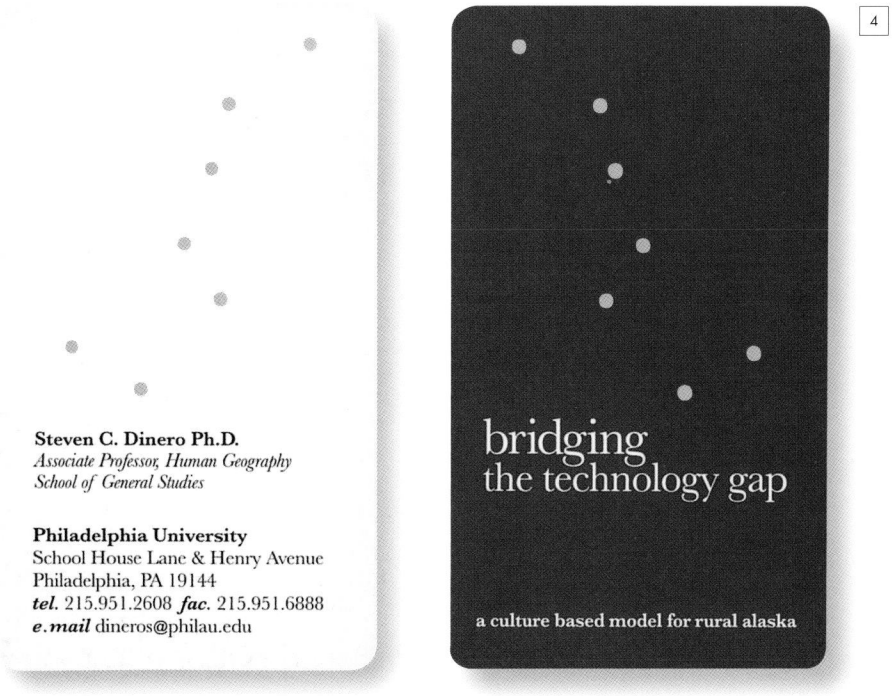

4

3

design firm: Sparc, Inc.
art director: Richard Cassis
designer: Richard Cassis
client: Yoga Laurie
software/hardware: Adobe Illustrator, InDesign, and Photoshop
paper/materials: Curious Collection Touch Soft Whipped Cream

4

design firm: Philadelphia University Design
art director: Frank Baseman
designer: Maria Ceara
client: Steven Dinero, Philadelphia University
software/hardware: Adobe Illustrator
paper/materials: Strathmore Cover, Offset printing with die-cuts

SHINE
ADVERTISING CO.

612 W. Main Street
Madison, WI 53703
SHINE ADVERTISING CO., LLC
P› 608 442 7373
F› 608 442 7374
WWW.SHINENORTH.COM
EMILIE SMITH
esmith@shinenorth.com

1

617
617
617
*461
*9677
www.jennaadams.com

JENNA ADAMS
stylist

2

3

4

1

design firm: Shine Advertising
art director: Miek Kriefski
designer: Peter Bell
client: Shine Advertising

2

design firm: Interrobang Design Collaborative
art director: Mark D. Sylvester
designer: Mark D. Sylvester
client: Jenna Adams, stylist
software/hardware: Adobe Illustrator CS2
paper/materials: Centura Gloss 100 lb cover gloss laminate

3

design firm: Entermotion Design Studio
designer: Lea Morrow
client: Avivo Brick Oven Pizza and In the Sauce Brands
software/hardware: Macromedia Freehand
paper/materials: Domtar Feltweave 3 color

4

design firm: Element
art director: Jeremy Slagle
client: Columbus Cutters
software/hardware: Adobe Photoshop, InDesign and Illustrator

1

1

design firm: Origami
art director: Michael Wou
illustrator: Michael Wou
client: Origami
software/hardware: Adobe InDesign

2

design firm: Popcorn Initiative
art director: Chris Jones
designer: Chris Jones
client: Popcorn Initiative
software/hardware: Adobe Illustrator
paper/materials: French Paper Steel Blue

3

design firm: BBM&D
designer: Barbara Brown
client: Jamal Edwards: The Genius Organization
software/hardware: Adobe Illustrator
paper/materials: Metal

POPCORN
INITIATIVE
CHRIS JONES
1602 Robin Road • Orlando, Florida 32803
Phone: 407-228-6601 • Fax: 407-228-9803
chris@popcorninitiative.com

2

THE GENIUS ORGANIZATION
Jamal Edwards
805.701.0952
go wireless go on.site go repair go secured

3

1

MELINDA FENTON
SAN FRANCISCO

MELINDA HENDERSON
PRESIDENT

P 415.567.8833 F 415.567.4216 E melinda@melindafenton.com

2

POLICY FIND
Insurance
ARCHEOLOGY SERVICES

POLICY FIND
Insurance
ARCHEOLOGY SERVICES

EMILY GONZALEZ
- Project Coordinator -
1060 N. CAPITOL AVENUE - SUITE E230
INDIANAPOLIS, INDIANA 46204

317.972.7870 P | F 317.972.7875
WWW.POLICYFIND.COM

3

4

1

design firm: Helena Seo Design
art director: Helena Seo
designer: Helena Seo
client: Melinda Fenton
software/hardware: Adobe Illustrator

2

design firm: Timber Design Co.
art director: Lars Lawson
client: PolicyFind
software/hardware: Adobe Photoshop, Macromedia Freehand, and Quark Xpress
paper/materials: Cougar Natural 100 lb cover

3

design firm: 3
art director: Sam Maclay
designer: Tim McGrath
client: Chez Nous
software/hardware: Quark Xpress and Adobe Illustrator
paper/materials: Domtar Paper

4

design firm: B.L.A. Design Company
art director: Brandi Lariscy Avant
designer: Brandi Lariscy Avant
illustrator: Brandi Lariscy Avant
client: B.L.A. Design Company
software/hardware: Adobe Illustrator CS
paper/materials: 2 match colors, letterpress, 2-ply museum board

1

David Reinker, AIA
President
dreinker@sgpa.com
SGPA ARCHITECTURE AND PLANNING
SAN DIEGO · SAN FRANCISCO
1545 HOTEL CIRCLE SOUTH, STUDIO 200
SAN DIEGO, CALIFORNIA 92108
P. 619.297.0131 F. 619.294.9534 WWW.SGPA.COM
RETAIL
SENIOR LIVING
EDUCATION
MIXED-USE

2

5151
santa fe street
suite h
san diego california
92109
www.sanpasqualwinery.com
SAN DIEGO
ORIGINAL
SAN PASQUAL
WINERY
STEVE MAY owner
tel 619 846 4163 fax 760 487 1065
steve@sanpasqualwinery.com

3

4

THE HENLEY COLLEGE LIBRARY

1

design firm: Blik
art director: Tyler Blik
designer: Yuki Hayashi
client: SGPA Architecture
software/hardware: Adobe CS
paper/materials: Beckett Enhance

2

design firm: Miriello Grafico
designer: Sallie Reynolds Allen
client: San Pasqual Winery
software/hardware: Adobe Illustrator

3

design firm: Alphabet Arm Design
art director: Aaron Belyea
designer: Ryan Frease
client: Tyrannosaurus Records
software/hardware: Adobe Illustrator

4

design firm: MBA
art director: Mark Brinkman and Mike Coffin
designer: Mark Brinkman
and Caroline Pledger
client: 2 Man Tour
software/hardware: Adobe Creative Suite
paper/materials: Neenah Classic Crest

MMIII
EP
3.14159...
EMERGENT PROPERTIES INC.

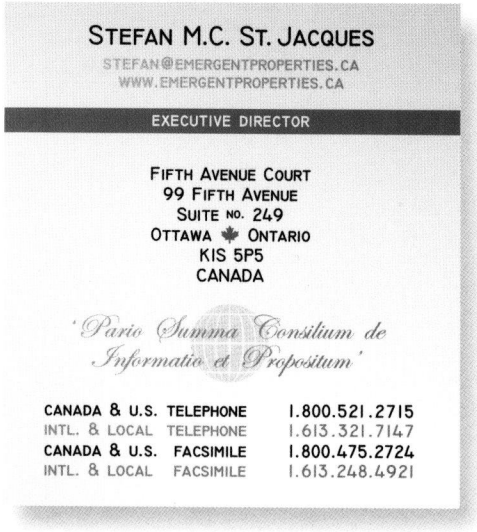
STEFAN M.C. ST. JACQUES
STEFAN@EMERGENTPROPERTIES.CA
WWW.EMERGENTPROPERTIES.CA
EXECUTIVE DIRECTOR
FIFTH AVENUE COURT
99 FIFTH AVENUE
SUITE NO. 249
OTTAWA ONTARIO
K1S 5P5
CANADA
'Pario Summa Consilium de Informatio et Propositum'
CANADA & U.S. TELEPHONE 1.800.521.2715
INTL. & LOCAL TELEPHONE 1.613.321.7147
CANADA & U.S. FACSIMILE 1.800.475.2724
INTL. & LOCAL FACSIMILE 1.613.248.4921

1

gina cartwright 713 818 8005
gina@charmed-circle.com
www.charmed-circle.com
charmedcircle

2

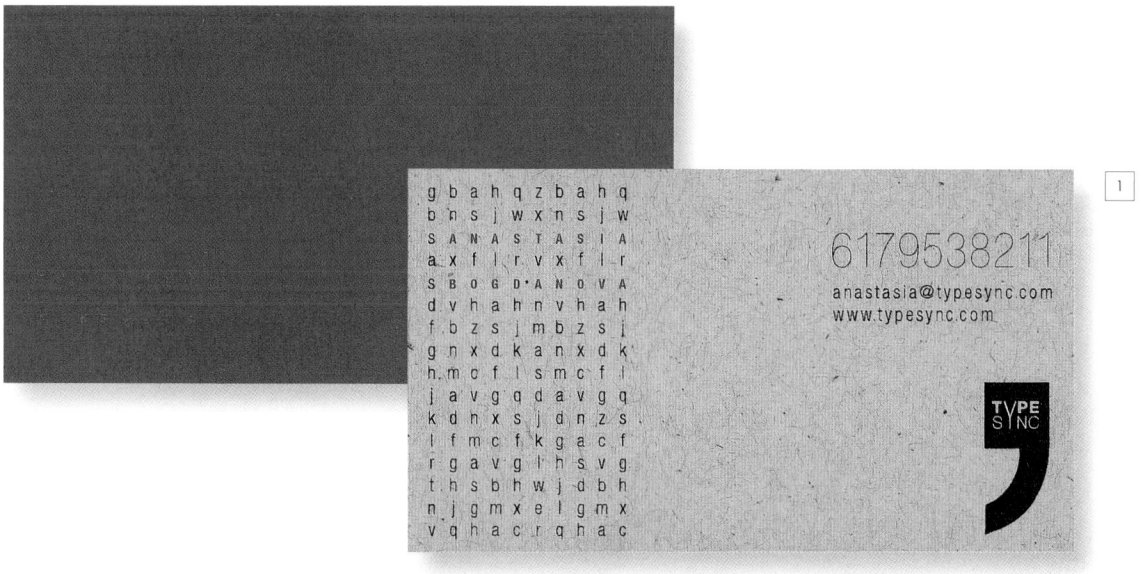
6179538211
anastasia@typesync.com
www.typesync.com
TYPE SYNC

1

Carey Kubik PRESIDENT
Small Town
TREASURES
8113 E OLD MILL COURT
WICHITA, KANSAS 67226
ph 316-744-0095
cell 316-641-8305
fax 316-744-1961
email
CAREY@SMALLTOWNTREASURESINC.COM
SMALLTOWNTREASURESINC.COM

2

3

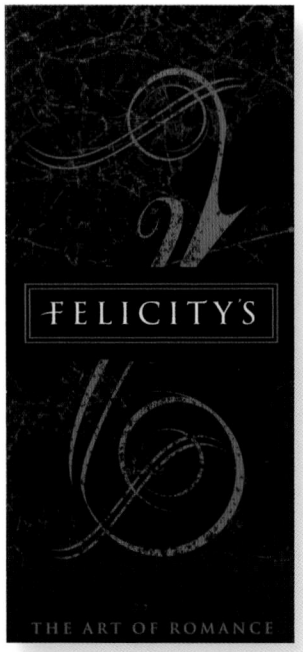

4

1

design firm: Miles Design
art director: Josh Miles
client: Simply She
software/hardware: Adobe Illustrator CS2
paper/materials: Cougar 100 lb White

2

design firm: Inovāt
art director: Doug Logan
designer: Sean Hennessey
client: Inovāt
software/hardware: Adobe Illustrator and Photoshop
paper/materials: Charcoal duplex and vellum

3

design firm: Willoughby Design Group
art director: Zack Shubkagel
and Ann Willoughby
(Creative director)
designer: Stephanie Lee
client: Feng

4

design firm: Greteman Group
art director: Sonia Greteman
designer: James Strange
client: Felicity's
(high-end lingerie, bath
and fragrance products)

317.570.5525
she@simplysheaffair.com
www.simplysheaffair.com
simply she
simply she

1

Justin Feagley
Business Development
justin@inovat.com
v: 717.367.5446
c: 717.201.4218
www.inovat.com
INOVĀT
INOVĀT

2

3

4

1

design firm: Emergent Properties
art director: Stefan M.C. St. Jacques
designer: Stefan M.C. St. Jacques
client: Emergent Properties

2

design firm: Limb Design
art director: Elise Desilva
designer: Emilie Desilva
client: Charmed Circle
software/hardware: Adobe InDesign
paper/materials: Paniere

3

design firm: Nothing: Something: NY
art director: Kevin Landwehr
designer: Kevin Landwehr and Devin Becker
client: Vinyl-Cut Music Management
paper/materials: Bockingford Triple-weight museum

4

design firm: Lotta Odelius Ord Bild Form
art director: Lotta Odelius
designer: Lotta Odelius
client: Lotta Odelius Ord Bild Form
software/hardware: Adobe Illustrator
paper/materials: Multi Design Original White (papyrus), matte laminate and spot-UV varnish (on one side).

3

4

1

design firm: Typesync Studio
art director: Anastasia Bogdanova
designer: Anastasia Bogdanova
client: Typesync Studio
software/hardware: Adobe Illustrator CS2
paper/materials: Domtar

2

design firm: Entermotion Design Studios
designer: Lea Morrow
client: Small Town Treasures
software/hardware: Macromedia Freehand
paper/materials: Neenah Classic Columns, 3 Color

3

design firm: MBA
art director: Mark Brinkman
designer: Caroline Pledger
illustrator: Nick Butcher
client: Cyan
software/hardware: Adobe Creative Suite
paper/materials: Strathmore Ultimate White

4

design firm: Entermotion Design Studio
designer: Lea Morrow
client: Barbed Wire Trucking
software/hardware: Macromedia Freehand

1

ARCCON CONSTRUCTION

Steve Arend President
543 W. Rich Street, Columbus, Ohio 43215
Tel 614.298.0430 Fax 614.298.0429 Cell 614.402.0344
sarend@arcconconstruction.com
www.arcconconstruction.com

ARCCON CONSTRUCTION

Jim Boggs Vice President
543 W. Rich Street, Columbus, Ohio 43215
Tel 614.298.0430 Fax 614.298.0429 Cell 614.402.0343
jboggs@arcconconstruction.com
www.arcconconstruction.com

ARCCON CONSTRUCTION

Steve Arend President
543 W. Rich Street, Columbus, Ohio 43215
Tel 614.298.0430 Fax 614.298.0429 Cell 614.402.0344
sarend@arcconconstruction.com
www.arcconconstruction.com

ARCCON CONSTRUCTION

Keith Scoby Superintendent
543 W. Rich Street, Columbus, Ohio 43215
Tel 614.298.0430 Fax 614.298.0429 Cell 614.419.4235
www.arcconconstruction.com

2

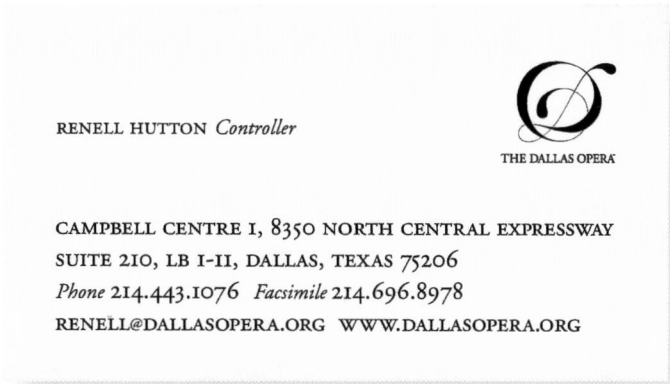

3

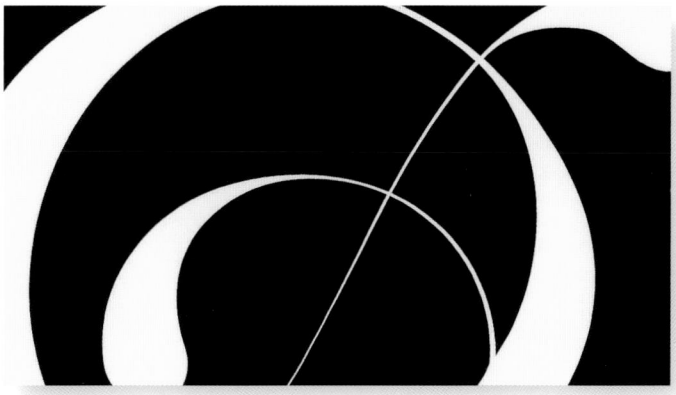

1

design firm: Base Art Co.
art director: Terry Rohrbach
designer: Terry Rohrbach
client: Arccon Construction
software/hardware: Adobe InDesign

2

design firm: KentLyons
art director: Kent Lyons
designer: Jon Cefai
client: KentLyons
software/hardware: Adobe Illustrator and InDesign

3

design firm: The Matchbox Studio
art director: Jeff Breazeale and Liz Burnett
designer: Jeff Breazeale and Liz Burnett
client: The Dallas Opera
paper/materials: Neenah Classic Crest

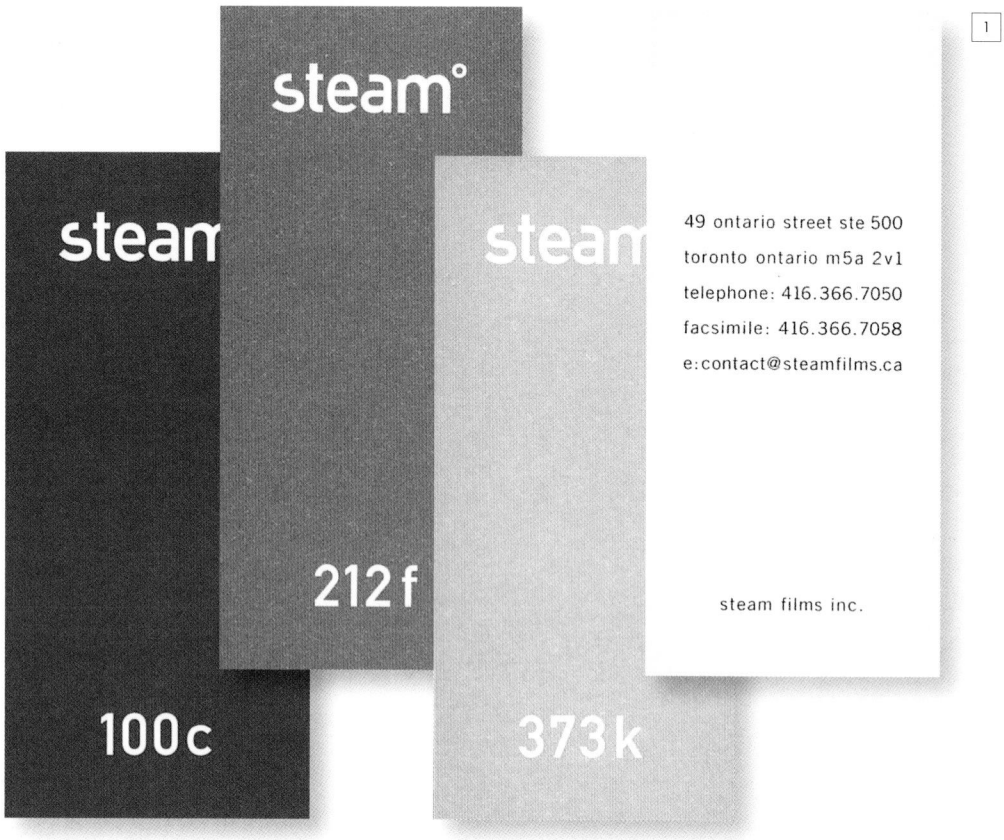
steam°
steam
steam
212f
100c
373k
49 ontario street ste 500
toronto ontario m5a 2v1
telephone: 416.366.7050
facsimile: 416.366.7058
e:contact@steamfilms.ca
steam films inc.

1

CARLA VILHENA FITNESS CONSULTANT
carla@energyfxfitness.com
310.429.7476
ENERGY F/X™
13428 MAXELLA AVE #717, MARINA DEL REY, CA 90292

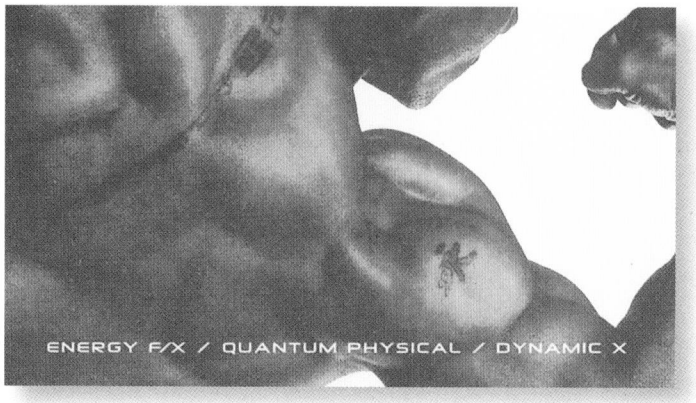
ENERGY F/X / QUANTUM PHYSICAL / DYNAMIC X

2

3

4

1

design firm: Blok
art director: Vanessa Eckstein
designer: Vanessa Eckstein and Frances Chen
client: Steam
software/hardware: Adobe Illustrator
paper/materials: Strathmore Ultimate White

2

design firm: Evenson Design
art director: Stan Evenson
designer: Melanie Usas
client: Energy FX
software/hardware: EPS

3

design firm: Sibley Peteet Design—Dallas
art director: Don Sibley
designer: Brandon Kirk
client: Commercial Investment Services
software/hardware: Adobe Illustrator
paper/materials: Mohawk Superfine Ultra-white Eggshell 130 double thick cover

4

design firm: Dottie Zimmerman, Maryville University student
art director: (Professor) Laurie Eisenbach-Bush
designer: Dottie Zimmerman, Maryville University student
client: Dottie Zimmerman, Maryville University student
software/hardware: Adobe Illustrator
paper/materials: Gilbert Clearfold 48 lb
printing: Epson Inkjet

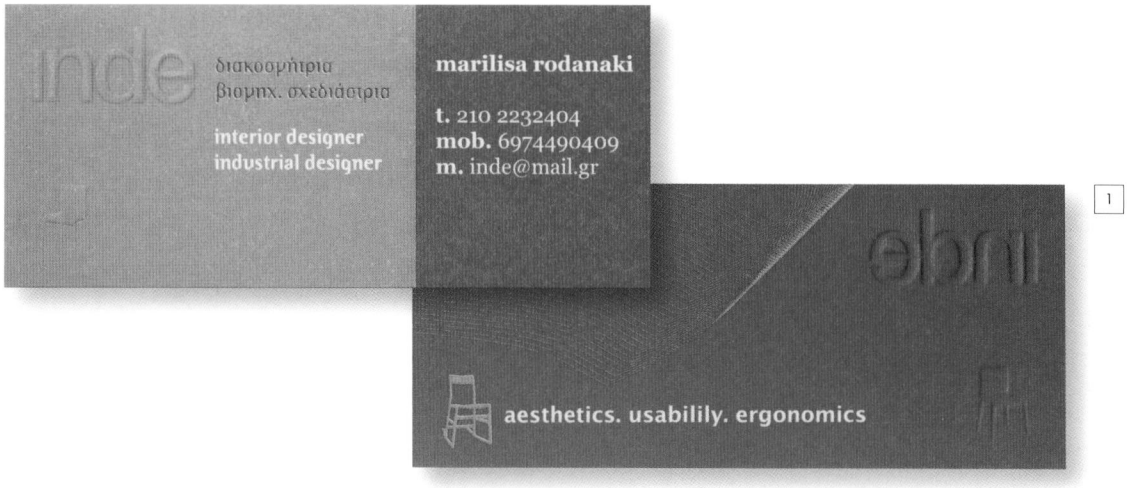
inde
διακοσμήτρια
βιομηχ. σχεδιάστρια
interior designer
industrial designer
marilisa rodanaki
t. 210 2232404
mob. 6974490409
m. inde@mail.gr
inde
aesthetics. usabilily. ergonomics

1

Lindsay McGarrahan ACCOUNT MANAGER
LINDSAY@BLUESHOEMARKETING.COM
1601 East 5th Street, Suite 109
Austin, Texas 78702
P: 512-473-2500 F: 512-320-5422
WWW.BLUESHOEMARKETING.COM
blue|shoe marketing
blue|shoe marketing

2

3

GAMBIT SOLUTIONS

info@gambitsolutions.com

610 Sixteenth Street #510
Oakland California 94612

510 808 4107 /Tel
510 808 4108 /Fax

business of IT

4

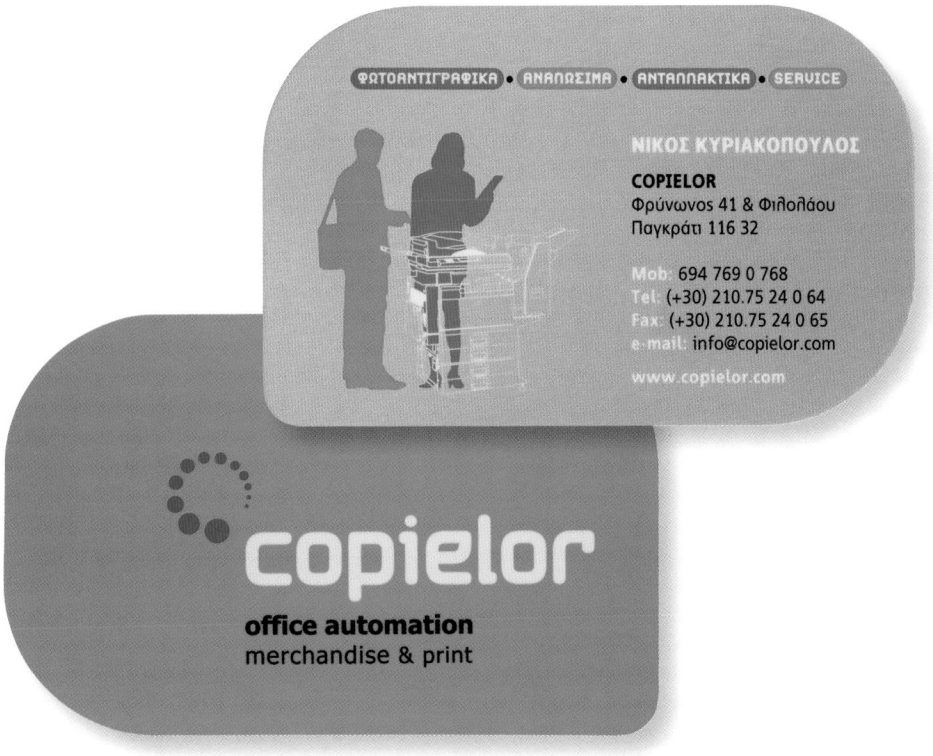

1

design firm: Di Depux
art director: Despina Bournele
designer: Despina Bournele
client: Marilisa Rodanaki
software/hardware: Adobe Illustrator CS
paper/materials: 2 Pantone, Zeta 250 gsm

2

design firm: Fangman Design
art director: Matt Fangman
designer: Matt Fangman
client: Blue Shoe Marketing
software/hardware: Adobe Illustrator
paper/materials: Classic Crest Solar White 100 lb cover

3

design firm: MINE™
art director: Christopher Simmons
designer: Christopher Simmons and Tim Belonax
client: Gambit Solutions
software/hardware: Adobe Illustrator CS2 and InDesign CS2
paper/materials: Mohawk Superfine Ultrawhite Smooth 130 lb DTC

4

design firm: Di Depux
art director: Despina Bournele
designer: Despina Bournele
client: Nikos Kyriakopoulos
software/hardware: Adobe Illustrator CS
paper/materials: 3 Pantone, Velvet finish

1

1

design firm: Originalia: A Design Studio
designer: Julie Mader-Meersman
illustrator: Julie Mader-Meersman
client: Originalia: A Design Studio
software/hardware: Adobe InDesign
paper/materials: Letterpress, French Durotone, one-of-a-kind collage

2

design firm: Reactor
art director: Clifton Alexander
designer: Chase Wilson
client: Reactor
software/hardware: Adobe Illustrator
paper/materials: Esse Arancio, 100 lb cover

3

design firm: Blue Sky Design
art director: Tom Hart
designer: Tom Hart
illustrator: Tom Hart
client: Tom Hart
software/hardware: Royal Typewriter
paper/materials: Gmund's Bier Paper, self-made rubber stamps, Archival "brilliance" pigment inkpad

REACTOR
YOUR CREATIVE ACCELERATOR
Clifton Alexander_president
816-841-3682
clifton@yourreactor.com
3111 Wyandotte, Suite 204, Kansas City, MO 64111

2

TomHart
Hartoon.com
718 783-4826
ArtDirector/Designer

№54321
718 207 4100
ArtDirector/Designer
REGISTERED

3

ORIGINAL
ArtDirector/Designer

PRINTED MATTER
TomHart
Hartoon.com
718 783-4826
ArtDirector/Designer

christiansen : creative
C
tricia christiansen
principal
tricia@christiansencreative.com

C
511 Second Street
Suite 206
Hudson, Wisconsin
54016
P 715 381 8480
F 715 381 8498
christiansen : creative
tricia christiansen
principal
tricia@christiansencreative.com

C
christiansen : creative
tricia christiansen
principal
tricia@christiansencreative.com
511 Second Street
Suite 206
Hudson, Wisconsin
54016
P 715 381 8480
F 715 381 8498

1

PURITY

INNOVATIVE WATER DESIGNS
info@puritywaterco.com
PH 317.863.2330
FX 317.863.2331
11252 Fall Creek Road
Indianapolis, IN 46256
puritywaterco.com

2

3

FSB DESIGN
FORMA&CONTEÚDO

WWW.FSBDESIGN.COM
11 3061 9596

FLÁVIO CARVALHO
DESIGNER

flavio.carvalho@fsb.com.br
11 8355 2249

r. pedroso alvarenga 900 7° andar
itaim bibi 04531 003
t. 11 3061.9596 f. 11 3086.0211

4

PURE SOURCE™

IT starts here.

NAME : HERBERT SAMUELS
TITLE : President

ADDRESS : 437 East 51 Street
Brooklyn, NY 11203

TELEPHONE : 347 365 2000
FACSIMILE : 360 365 2003

EMAIL : h.samuels@puresource.net
WEBSITE : www.puresource.com

1

design firm: Christiansen: Creative
designer: Tricia Christiansen
client: Christiansen: Creative
software/hardware: Quark Xpress
paper/materials: Fox River Sundance Felt

2

design firm: Miles Design
art director: Josh Miles
designer: Eric Folzenlogel
client: Purity Water Designs
software/hardware: Adobe Illustrator CS
paper/materials: 110 lb white cover/die

3

design firm: FSB Design
art director: Dora Medonça
and Flávio Carvalho
designer: Flávio Carvalho
client: FSB Design
software/hardware: Adobe Illustrator CS
paper/materials: dull couche, varnish stamp

4

design firm: 3rd Edge Communications
art director: Frankie Gonzalez
designer: Melissa Medina Mackin
client: Pure Source

AMY JO JURSICH, *designer*
3323 NORTH PAULINA NUMBER 2D
CHICAGO ILLINOIS 60657
T/F 773.525.9001 AJJURSICH@MSN.COM

1

2

3

1

design firm: Pagliuco Design Company
art director: Michael Pagliuco

2

design firm: Ana Roncha
art director: Ana Roncha

3

design firm: Turnstyle
art director: Ben Graham

1

après peau

TINA ALSTER, M.D.
PROPRIETOR

LIBERTY JONES
manager

1430 K STREET NW | WASHINGTON, DC 20005 | 202.783.0022
www.aprespeau.com

2

3

1

design firm: Willoughby Design Group
art director: Nicole Satterwhite and (Creative directors) Ann Willoughby and Megan Semrick

2

design firm: Meagan Goldberg
art director: Meagan Goldberg
designer: Meagan Goldberg
client: Meagan Goldberg
software/hardware: Adobe Illustrator CS, MAC

3

design firm: Substância 4 Comunicação e Design
art director: Carolina Terra and Marcia Albuquerque
designer: Marcia Albuquerque and Carolina Terra

1

Suzanne Holzworth
PRINTMAKER
suzanne@worthitstudio.com
www.worthitstudio.com

Suzanne Holzworth
PRINTMAKER
suzanne@worthitstudio.com
www.worthitstudio.com

Suzanne Holzworth
PRINTMAKER
suzanne@worthitstudio.com
www.worthitstudio.com

2

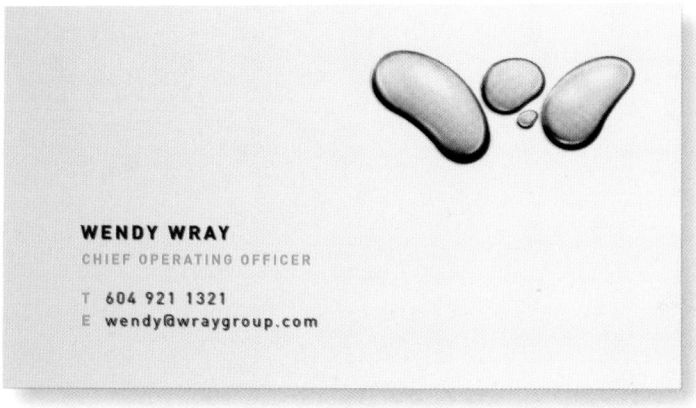

3

1

design firm: Bennett Holzworth Design
art director: Bennett Holzworth
client: Suzanne Holzworth: Printmaker
software/hardware: Adobe Illustrator, InDesign, and Photoshop
paper/materials: Online Postcard printer, hand letterpress

2

design firm: Element
art director: John McCollum
designer: Megan Graham
client: Nvest Wealth Strategies
software/hardware: Adobe InDesign

3

design firm: Dossier Creative, Inc.
art director: Don Chisholm
designer: Patrick Smith
client: Wray Consulting Group
software/hardware: Adobe Illustrator and InDesign
paper/materials: Laminated Topkote 78 lb dull cover

jungeschachtel
Kleiner aufmachen
chachtel.de

1

1

design firm: Jungeschachtel
art director: Nina Dautzenberg and Andrea Gadesmann
client: Jungeschachtel

THE
MONTGOMERY
EST. 1914

74 NEW MONTGOMERY STREET SAN FRANCISCO, CA 94105
Telephone
Facsimile
Website
415 512 7474
415 512 7575
THEMONTGOMERYSF.COM

1

bolings
plaza board of trade
4800 main street
kansas city missouri 64112
t - 816.753.1718
gateway plaza
9055 metcalf avenue
overland park kansas 66212
t - 913.341.1718
orchard corner center
9576 quivira road
lenexa kansas 66215
t - 913.888.6618
w - www.bolings.com
BO LINGS
chinese please!
BO LINGS
chinese please!

2

3

4

1

design firm: Bakken Creative Co.
art director: Michelle Bakken
designer: Gina Mondello and Tae Hatayama
client: Pacific Marketing Associates
software/hardware: Adobe Illustrator

2

design firm: Design Ranch
art director: Michelle Sonderegger and Ingred Sidie
designer: Michelle Sonderegger and Ingred Sidie
client: Bo Lings
software/hardware: Adobe Illustrator

3

design firm: Archrival
art director: Clint! Runge
designer: Clint! Runge
client: Nomad Lounge
software/hardware: Adobe Illustrator CS2

4

design firm: Crave, Inc.
art director: David Edmundson
designer: David Edmundson
client: Sienna Graphics

1

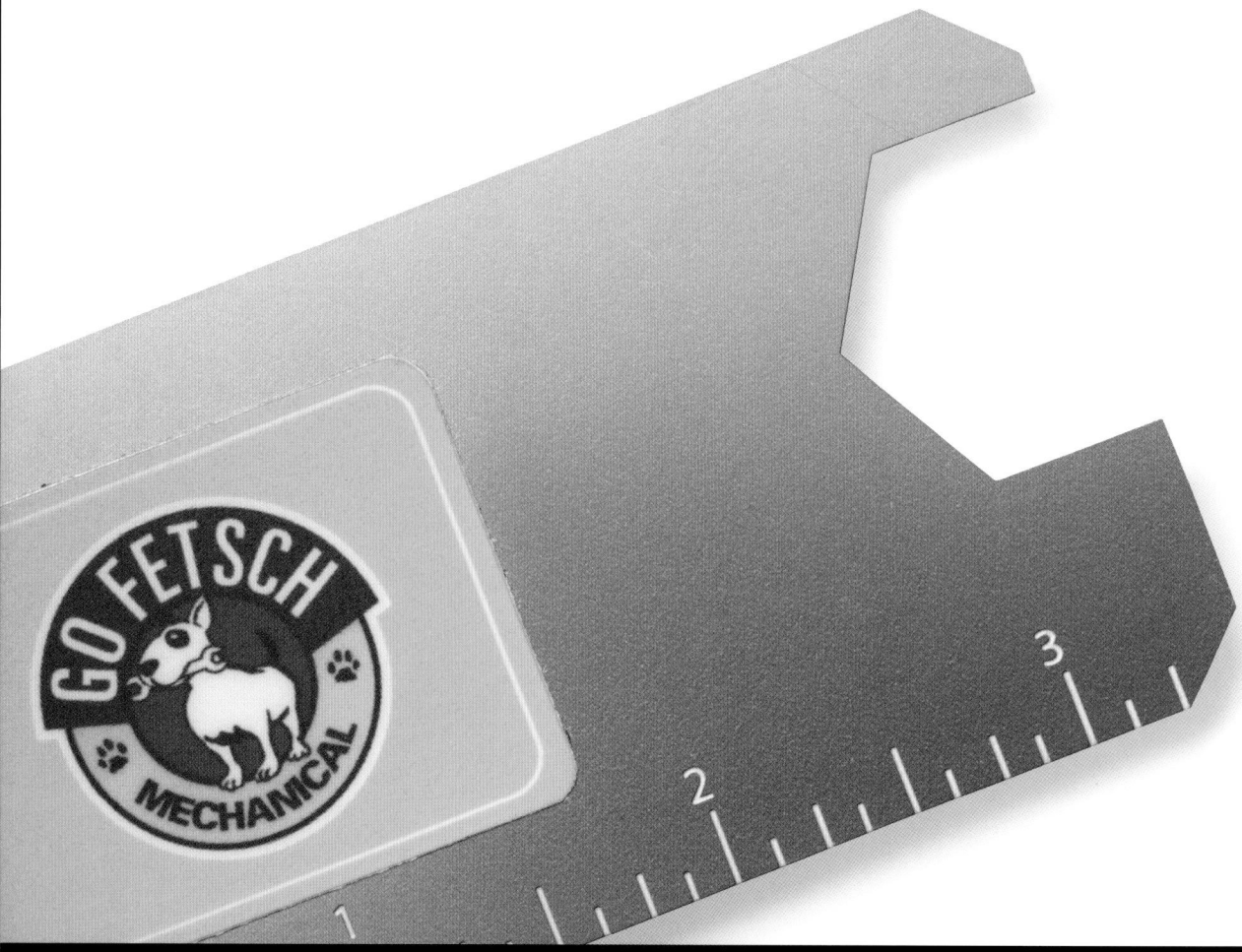

1

design firm: Red Circle Agency
art director: Matt Benka
designer: Bryan Dunn
client: Go Fetsch Mechanical

2

design firm: MINE™
art director: Christopher Simmons
designer: Christopher Simmons
client: Steel Media

3

design firm: smashLAB
art director: Eric Karjaluoto
designer: Robert Young
client: NUGSS

2

RICHARD STEEL
President
NY/ 917 405 8590
LA/ 310 346 3455
rich@steelmediainc.com
STEEL MEDIA
49 West 69th Street Suite 2A
New York NY 10023
www.steelmediainc.com

3

Simone Renaud
Ombudsperson
nugss
UNBC Northern Undergraduate Student Society
3333 University Way, Prince George, BC, V2N 4Z9
T. 250.960.6427 F. 250.960.5617
E. ombuds@nugss.com
www.nugss.com

1
SK+G
skgadv.com
Stephen Averitt
Executive Design Director
T 702 478 4000 F 702 478 4001
steve.averitt@skgadv.com
8912 Spanish Ridge Avenue
Las Vegas, Nevada 89148
SK+G
MEMO
8912 Spanish Ridge Avenue
Las Vegas, Nevada 89148
T 702 478 4000 F 702 478 4001

2
realitydigital
Cynthia Francis / CEO
600 Townsend St, Ste 170e, San Francisco, CA 94103
415.503.3959 o / 415.760.4717 m / 415.437.2892 f
www.realitydigital.com / cfrancis@realitydigital.com

3

4

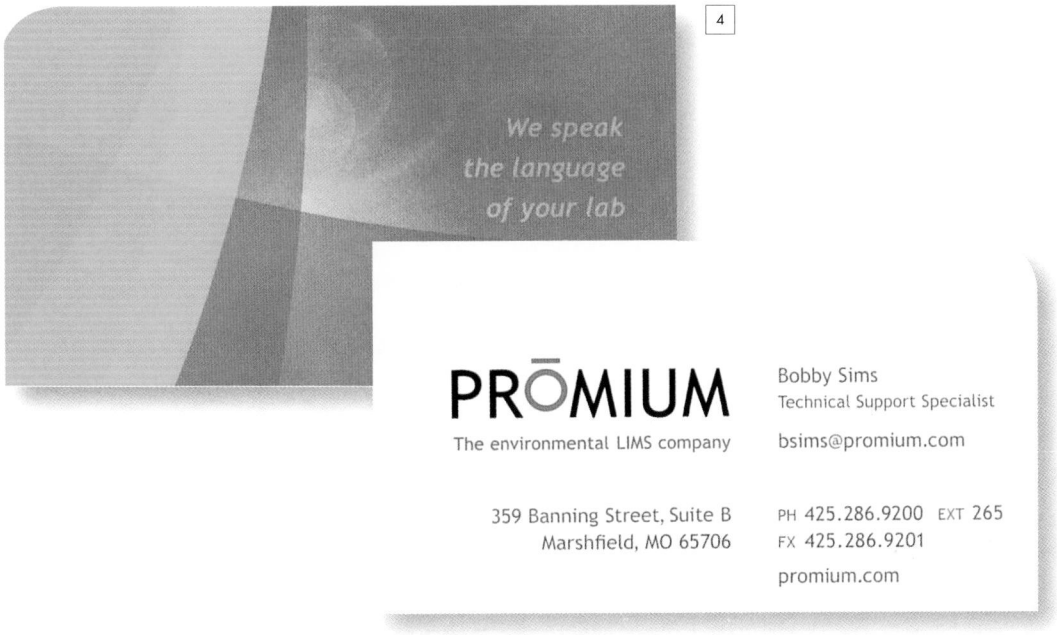

1

design firm: SK+G Advertising
art director: Steve Averitt
designer: Ralwa Lee
client: SK+G Advertising
software/hardware: Adobe Illustrator and InDesign
paper/materials: Mohawk Navajo

2

design firm: Helena Seo Design
art director: Helena Seo
designer: Helena Seo
client: Reality Digital
software/hardware: Adobe Illustrator
paper/materials: Starwhite Sirius Smooth 130 lb DTC

3

design firm: Imagine
art director: David Caunce
designer: David Caunce
client: Travelbeam
software/hardware: Adobe Illustrator
paper/materials: Conqueror CX22

4

design firm: Belyea
art director: Ron Lars Hansen
designer: Ron Lars Hansen
client: Promium
software/hardware: Adobe Illustrator and InDesign
paper/materials: Neenah Environment

1

INSTITUT DU LASER CUTANÉ DE L'OUTAOUAIS
200, rue Montcalm, bureau 302, Gatineau (Québec) J8Y 3B5

ILCO

2

ultra_DESIGN

braulio lacerda carollo
braulio@ultradesign.com.br

rua padre anchieta 2454
conjunto 503
curitiba 80730 000

www.ultradesign.com.br
ultra@ultradesign.com.br

41 3016 3023

DESIGNYEMLEL
$19.86
1 20628 56900 7
Lemley Design is a leader in branded customer experience at retail.
LEMLEY DESIGN CAN BE BLEACHED IF NEEDED, DRY FLAT
LEMLEYNGISED
DIANA FRYC Director of Business Development
ADDRESS 2727 FAIRVIEW AVE. E, SUITE F, SEATTLE, WA 98102, USA
TELEPHONE 206 285 6900 x202 / FACSIMILE 206 285 6906
INTERNET www.lemleydesign.com / EMAIL diana@lemleydesign.com

3

SELTZER
design intelligence
rochelle seltzer, AIGA ○ president
SELTZER 45 Newbury Street, Suite 406 | Boston MA 02116
617 353 0303t | 617 262 0255f | seltzerdesign.com | rs@seltzerdesign.com

4

1

1

design firm: Bennett Holzworth Design
art director: Bennett Holzworth
client: Be a Design Group
software/hardware: Adobe Illustrator, InDesign, and Photoshop
paper/materials: Letterpress, stickers, photopolymer plates, Neenah Eames

A GRAPHIC DESIGN BLOG
BE A DESIGN GROUP
Adrian Hanft
adrian@beadesigngroup.com
www.beadesigngroup.com
A GRAPHIC DESIGN BLOG
BE A DESIGN GROUP
Bennett Holzworth
bennett@beadesigngroup.com
www.beadesigngroup.com
A GRAPHIC DESIGN BLOG
BE A DESIGN GRO
Bennett Holzwort

DEED
João José Guerreiro
Agente Comercial
Rua Nova · 420 · Gestrins
4570 - 074 Balasar · PVZ
T 252 955 190
M 962 612 526
E info@deed.pt
W www.deed.pt

1

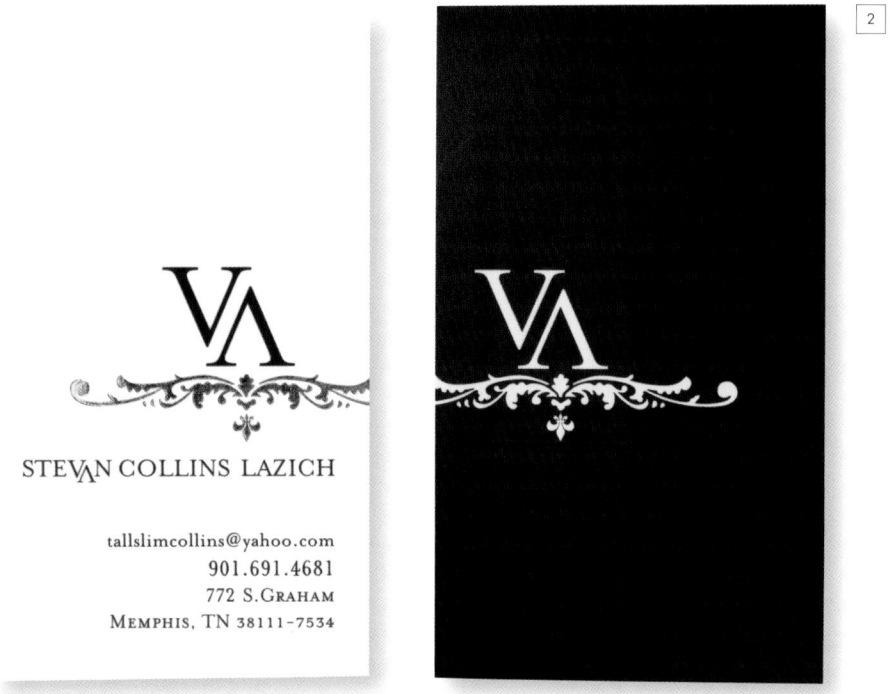
VA
STEVAN COLLINS LAZICH
tallslimcollins@yahoo.com
901.691.4681
772 S.Graham
Memphis, TN 38111-7534
VA

2

3

1

design firm: Ana Roncha
art director: Ana Roncha
designer: Ana Roncha
client: DEED
software/hardware: Macromedia Freehand and Adobe Illustrator CS
paper/materials: Couché Date with varnish on one side

2

design firm: Switch Creative
art director: Michael Carpenter
designer: Michael Carpenter
client: SteVan Lazich
software/hardware: Adobe Illustrator
paper/materials: Silk cards and foil

3

design firm: Miles Design
art director: Josh Miles
designer: Eric Folzenlogel
client: Harmony X: United Artists of Expodesign
software/hardware: Adobe Illustrator CS2
paper/materials: French Cement 100 lb

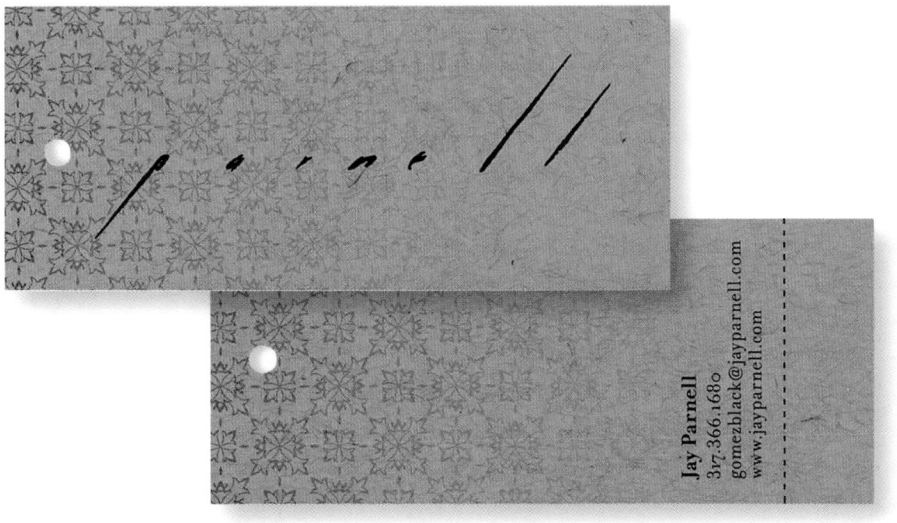

4

4

design firm: Miles Design
art director: Josh Miles
designer: Eric Folzenlogel
client: Jay Parnell
software/hardware: Adobe Illustrator CS2
paper/materials: French Kraft 100 lb, thermo die-cut

ANA PAULA RODRIGUES
DIRECTORA ADMINISTRATIVA
RUA FERNÃO VAZ DOURADO 62
4150-322 PORTO PORTUGAL
T +351 226 165 569
F +351 226 165 570
E ana.paula@ska.pt
www.ska.pt
SKA
JORGE JORGE
HEAD OF DESIGN
RUA FERNÃO VAZ DOURADO 62
4150-322 PORTO PORTUGAL
T +351 226 165 571
F +351 226 165 570
M +351 969 508 795
E jorge.jorge@ska.pt
www.ska.pt
SKA
LUIS MAGNO
DIRECTOR DE PRODUÇÃO
RUA FERNÃO VAZ DOURADO 62
4150-322 PORTO PORTUGAL
T +351 226 165 563
F +351 226 165 570
M +351 969 508 793
E luis.magno@ska.pt
www.ska.pt

1

2

3

1

design firm: SKA
art director: Jorge Jorge
designer: Jorge Jorge
client: SKA
software/hardware: Freehand
paper/materials: Couche Date and Verniz

2

design firm: BR
art director: Franklin Oviedo, Anthony Magliano, Krista Masilionis, and Chuck Hoffman
designer: Franklin Oviedo and Anthony Magliano
writer: Brent Anderson
client: Bernstein-Rein Advertising
software/hardware: Adobe Illustrator and Photoshop
paper/materials: Classic Crest Natural

3

design firm: BR
art director: Franklin Oviedo, Anthony Magliano, Krista Masilionis, and Chuck Hoffman
designer: Franklin Oviedo and Anthony Magliano
writer: Brent Anderson
client: Rush Wade 2 Photography
software/hardware: Adobe Illustrator and Photoshop
paper/materials: Classic Crest Natural

KENNETH'S
YOUR NEXT APPOINTMENT IS:
DATE
TIME
WITH
EMAIL
KENNETH'S
KENNETH'S
KENNETH'S
KENNETH'S
LOOK GOOD.
KENNETH SMITH
OWNER
2100 ST. CHARLES AVE.
NEW ORLEANS LA 70130
504.528.8585
400 VETERANS BLVD.
METAIRIE LA 70005
504.833.5556

1

1305 e 15th suite 202
tulsa ok 74120
918 295 0044
fax 918 295 0055
davidclarkDESIGN
becky gelder
bg@davidclarkdesign.com
www.davidclarkdesign.com

2

3

4

1

design firm: Zande + Newman Design
art director: Adam Newman
designer: Jan Bertman and Loren Stephens
client: Kenneth's Studio for Hair
software/hardware: Adobe InDesign
paper/materials: Mohawk Superfine

2

design firm: David Clark Design
art director: David Clark
designer: Becky Gelder
client: David Clark Design
software/hardware: Adobe Illustrator CS
paper/materials: Classic Crest Solar White 80 lb cover, Fasson
printing: Western Printing

3

design firm: AngryPorcupine*Design
art director: Cheryl Roder-Quill
designer: Cheryl Roder-Quill
client: Cheryl Dailey Makeup and Hair
software/hardware: Adobe Illustrator
paper/materials: Curious Metallics; 1 PMS and black
printing: Carr Printing Company (Bountiful, UT)

4

design firm: 3
art director: Sam Maclay
designer: Tim McGrath
illustrator: Tim McGrath
client: Measure Twice
software/hardware: Quark Xpress and Adobe Illustrator
paper/materials: French Paper and printed labels

1

2

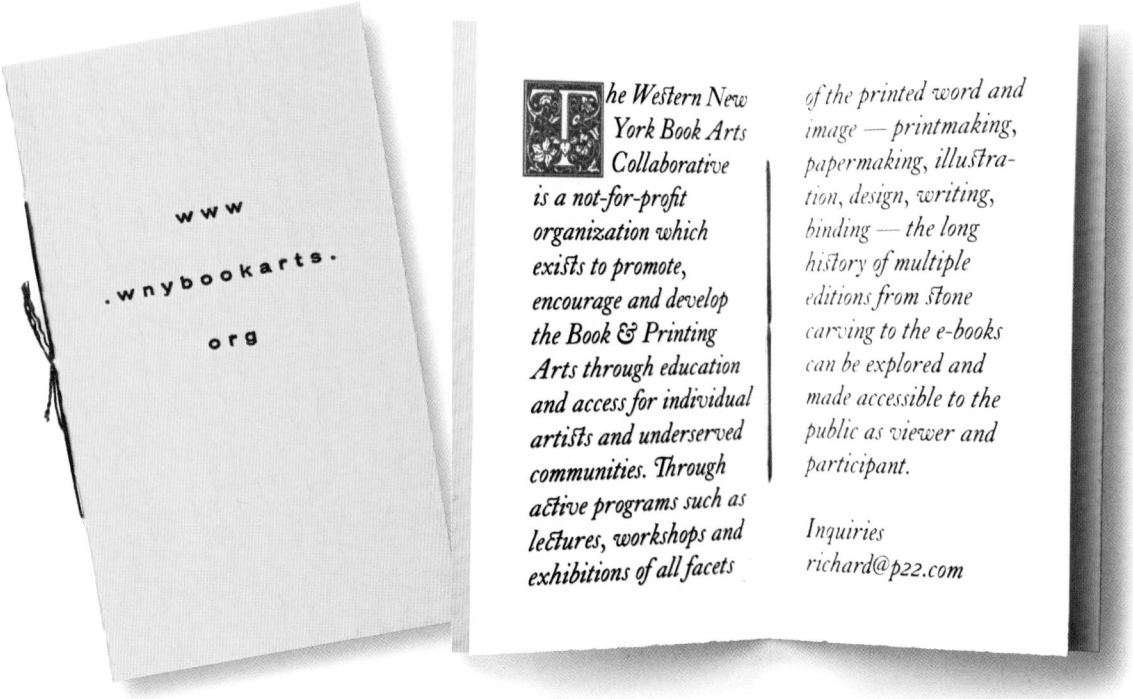

1

design firm: Crave, Inc.
art director: David Edmundson
designer: David Edmundson
client: Sienna Graphics

2

design firm: P22
art director: Richard Kegler
designer: Richard Kegler
client: WNY Book Arts Collaborative
software/hardware: Adobe InDesign

3

design firm: JSDS
art director: JSDS
designer: Justin Skeesuck
client: JSDS
software/hardware: Adobe Illustrator

3

JSDS JSkeesuck Dsgn Std
Justin Skeesuck
7630 Marie Avenue
La Mesa California 91941
Call 619 277 2585
Email hello@jsds.us
Visit www.jsds.us
POSTCARD
Skeesuck D
Skeesuck
arie Avenue
a California 91941
277 2585
ello@jsds.us
ww.jsds.us
FOR ADDRESS ONLY
MAR
Best Birthd
Wis
Skeesuck Ds
Justin Skeesuck
7630 Marie Avenue
La Mesa California
Call 619 277 2585
Email hello@jsds.us
Visit www.jsds.us
- NAPOLI - Via Caracciolo con mare agitat

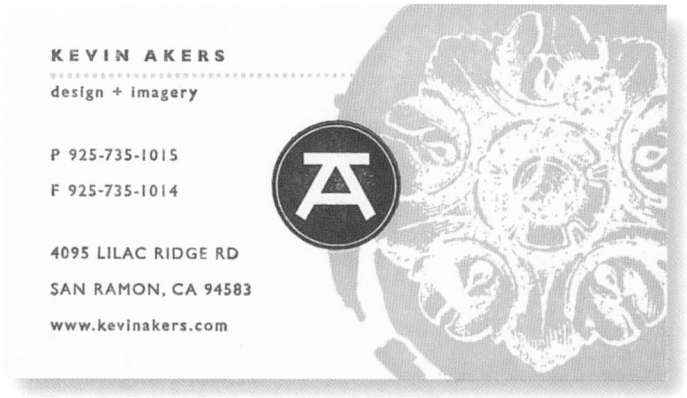
KEVIN AKERS
design + imagery
P 925-735-1015
F 925-735-1014
4095 LILAC RIDGE RD
SAN RAMON, CA 94583
www.kevinakers.com

1

RIVER BLUFF
[architects]

2

RONALD D. FUSTON, AIA
[1214 FREDERICK AVE ST JOSEPH MO 64501]
TEL 816 232 7248 FAX 816 233 3319
E-MAIL RFUSTON@RIVERBLUFF.COM

3

1

design firm: Kevin Akers Design and Imagery
art director: Kevin Akers
designer: Kevin Akers
illustrator: Kevin Akers
client: Kevin Akers
software/hardware: Adobe Illustrator
paper/materials: letterpress

2

design firm: Design Ranch
art director: Michelle Sonderegger and Ingred Sidie
designer: Michelle Sonderegger and Ingred Sidie
client: River Bluff
software/hardware: Adobe Illustrator

alex coletti
ph: 212 654 5091
fx: 212 654 9287
alex.coletti@mtvstaff.com

770 Broadway
New York NY 10003

alex coletti
productions

4

3

design firm: Dossier Creative, Inc.
art director: Don Chisholm
designer: Patrick Smith
client: Vincor International
software/hardware: Adobe Illustrator and InDesign
paper/materials: Laminated paper:
Front: Tomahawk, cool white 80 lb cover;
Back: Topkote 78 lb dull cover

4

design firm: Think Studio, NYC
art director: John Clifford
designer: John Clifford
illustrator: John Clifford
client: Alex Coletti Productions
software/hardware: Adobe Photoshop and Illustrator, Quark Xpress
paper/materials: Mohawk Superfine

Ace Architects
330 2nd Street, no1
Oakland, CA 94607
(510) 452-0775
www.aceland.com

1

SNAFU RESOLUTION
NICHE IDENTIFICATION
GIST ENHANCEMENT
///// *eric kass : utilitarian + commercial + fine : art //
// *indianapolis indiana . united states of america /////
///.*ring 317 590 5355 *visit. /// WWW.FUNNEL.TV
FUNNEL

2

3

4

1

design firm: Ace Architects
art director: Adam Gillett
designer: Adam Gillett
client: Ace Architects
software/hardware: Photoshop
paper/materials: Coated

2

design firm: Funnel: Eric Kass: Utilitarian + Commercial + Fine: Art
art director: Eric Kass
designer: Eric Kass
client: Funnel
software/hardware: Adobe Illustrator CC
paper/materials: Process Offset on Coated White cover with film laminate

3

design firm: Another Limited Rebellion
art director: Noah Scalin
designer: Noah Scalin
client: Ram Bhagat–Kevala Massage Therapy
software/hardware: Adobe Illustrator
paper/materials: Genesis Marigold

4

design firm: Dotzero Design
designer: Karen Wippich and Jon Wippich
client: Lieto
software/hardware: Adobe Illustrator and Photoshop
paper/materials: Cougar 80 lb cover

1

PROLIFIQ
Jim Van Kerkhove
Prolifiq Software
4145 SW Watson Ave.
Suite 450
Beaverton, OR 97005
E jimv@prolifiq.net
O +1 503 684 1415
M +1 503 539 1415
W www.prolifiq.net

GIANTANT

2

WENDY OWEN
PRINCIPAL
300 BRANNAN STREET NO.406
SAN FRANCISCO CALIFORNIA 94107
T 415 227 4235 F 415 227 4261
WENDY@GIANTANT.COM

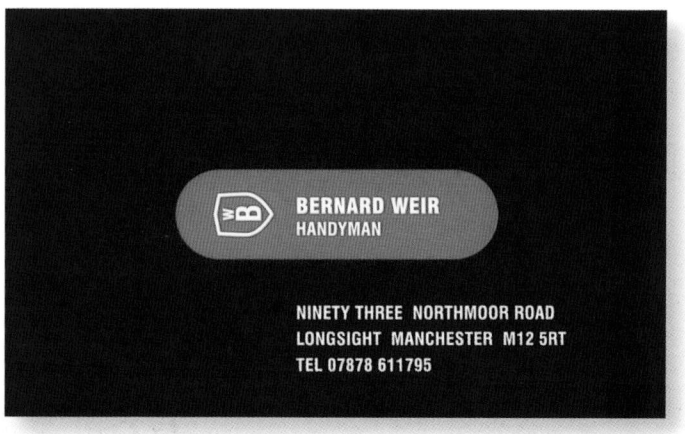
BERNARD WEIR
HANDYMAN
NINETY THREE NORTHMOOR ROAD
LONGSIGHT MANCHESTER M12 5RT
TEL 07878 611795

3

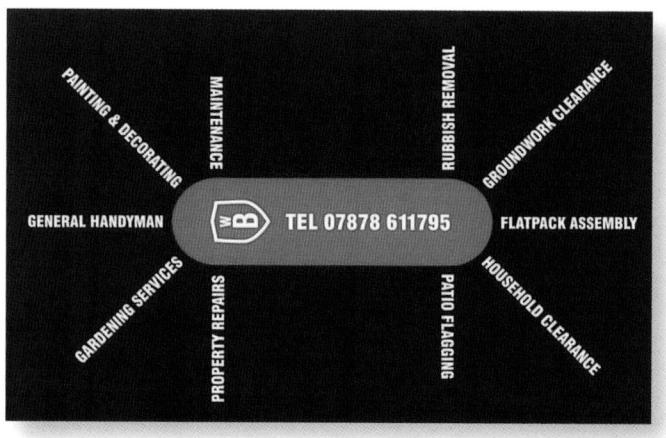
PAINTING & DECORATING
MAINTENANCE
RUBBISH REMOVAL
GROUNDWORK CLEARANCE
GENERAL HANDYMAN
TEL 07878 611795
FLATPACK ASSEMBLY
GARDENING SERVICES
PROPERTY REPAIRS
PATIO FLAGGING
HOUSEHOLD CLEARANCE

4

1

design firm: Liquid Agency
art director: Alfredo Muccino
designer: Jeff Gardner
client: Prolifiq
software/hardware: Adobe Illustrator

2

design firm: MINE™
art director: Christopher Simmons
designer: Christopher Simmons and Nancy Chew
client: Giant Ant
software/hardware: Adobe Illustrator CS2, Adobe InDesign CS2
paper/materials: 120 lb Neenah Eames Furniture White DTC

3

design firm: Imagine
art director: David Caunce
designer: David Caunce
client: Bernard Wier
software/hardware: Adobe Illustrator
paper/materials: Gloss and Matte Lamination, 300 gsm

4

design firm: Wyld Stallions
art director: Jason Arber
designer: Jason Arber
client: Wyld Stallions
software/hardware: Adobe Illustrator and InDesign CS2
paper/materials: 350 gsm Satin Board

1

1

design firm: Firebelly Design
art director: Dawn Hancock
designer: Dawn Hancock and Katie Yates
client: Awakening Organics
software/hardware: Adobe Illustrator and Photoshop

2

design firm: Turnstyle
art director: Ben Graham
designer: Ben Graham
client: Turquoise
software/hardware: Adobe Illustrator

3

design firm: EPOS, Inc.
art director: Gabrielle Raumberger
designer: Brandon Fall
client: Renufuel
software/hardware: Adobe Illustrator

2

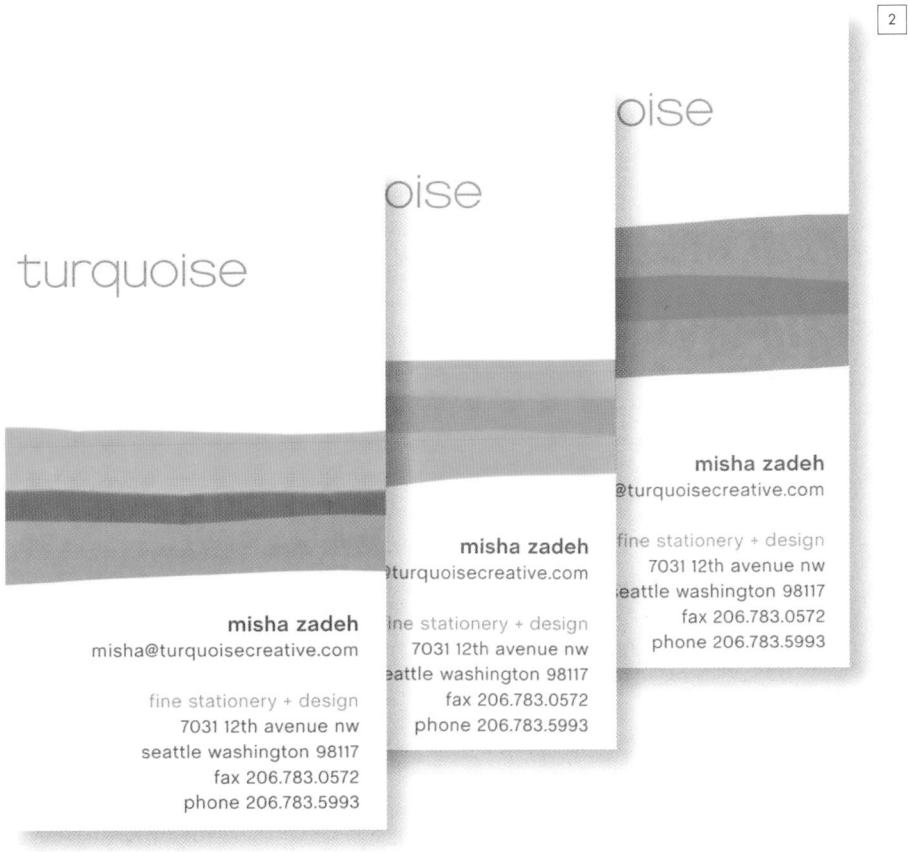

3

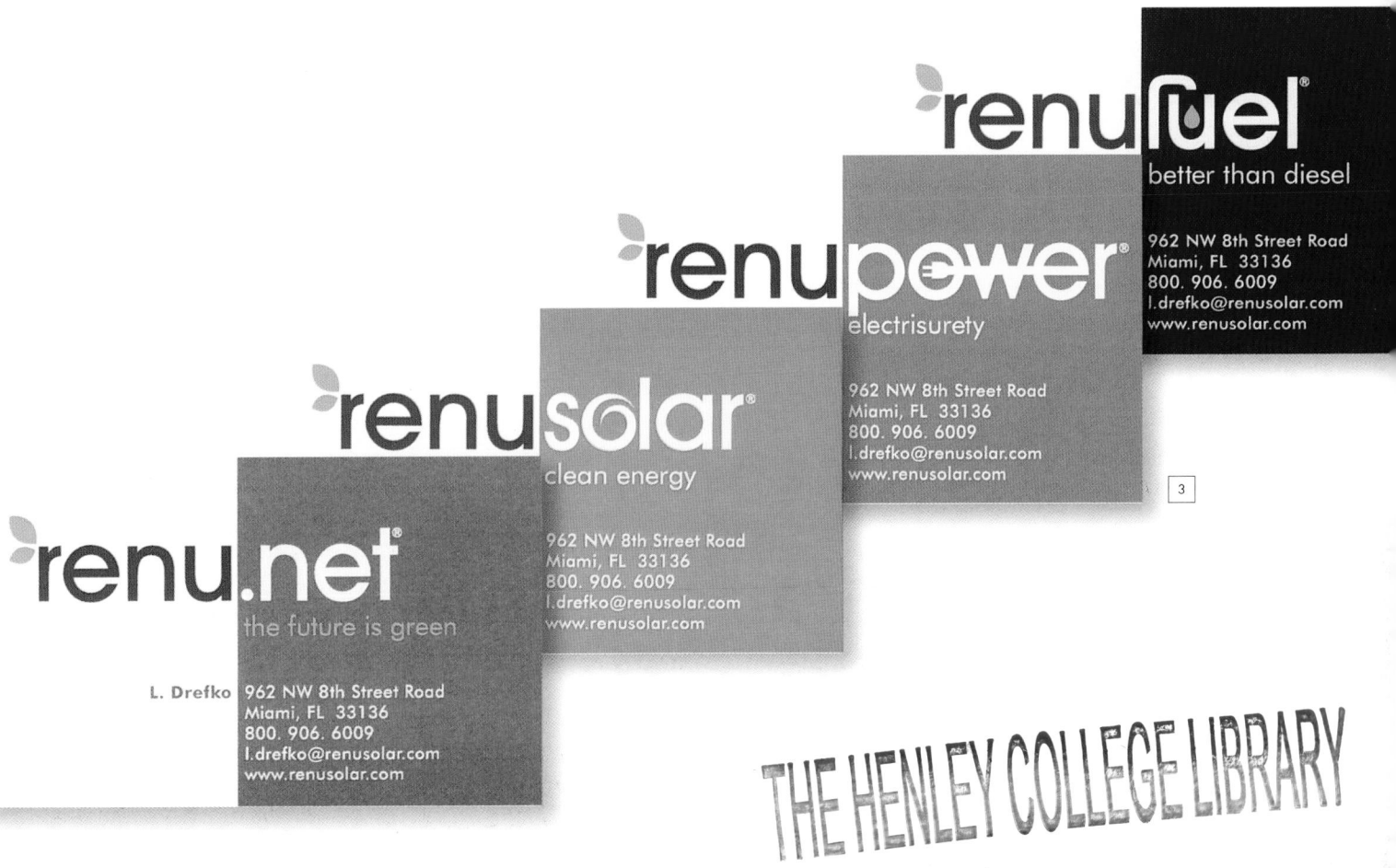

THE HENLEY COLLEGE LIBRARY

1

Suzanne Boccalatte Design Director

Telephone 61 2 9310 4309 I Mobile 0412 050 090
PO Box 370 Surry Hills NSW 2010 Sydney Australia
Studio 43. 61 Marlborough St Surry Hills NSW 2010
suzanne@boccalatte.com I boccalatte.com

bocca
-latte

2

3

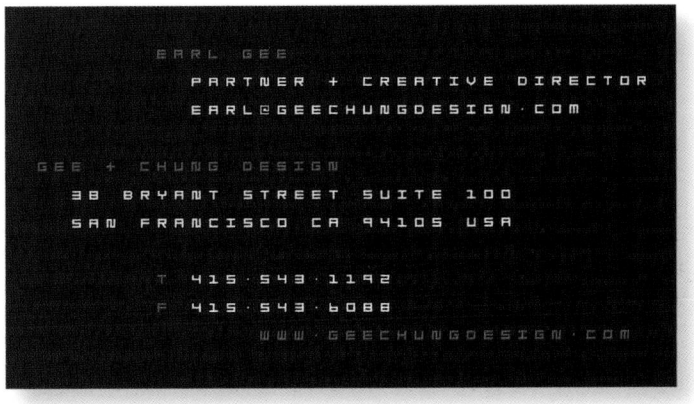

4

1

design firm: Boccalatte
art director: Suzanne Boccalatte
designer: Suzanne Boccalatte
client: Boccalatte
software/hardware: Adobe Illustrator and InDesign CS
paper/materials: Knight Smooth Cream, Verco type 350 gsm

2

design firm: Color Cubic
art director: Michael John and Christy Lai
designer: Christy Lai
client: Color Cubic
software/hardware: Adobe Illustrator and InDesign
paper/materials: Silk Laminate

3

design firm: Subplot Design, Inc.
art director: Matthew Clark and Roy White
designer: Matthew Clark
client: Change Advertising
software/hardware: Adobe Illustrator
paper/materials: Mohawk Options

4

design firm: Gee + Chung Design
art director: Earl Gee
designer: Earl Gee
client: Gee + Chung Design
software/hardware: Adobe Illustrator and InDesign
paper/materials: Mohawk Superfine 130 lb cover

RAGAS
Ιωάννης Κ. Ραγκαβάς
Κ. +30 6974 913997
info@e-ragas.com | www.e-ragas.com
require
assistance
get
appropriate
support

RAGAS
ΠΥΣΕΙΣ ΜΗΧΑΝΟΓΡΑΦΗΣΗΣ
ΠΑΡΟΧΗ ΥΠΗΡΕΣΙΩΝ ΠΛΗΡΟΦΟΡΙΚΗΣ
ΣΥΜΒΟΥΛΕΥΤΙΚΕΣ ΥΠΗΡΕΣΙΕΣ

1

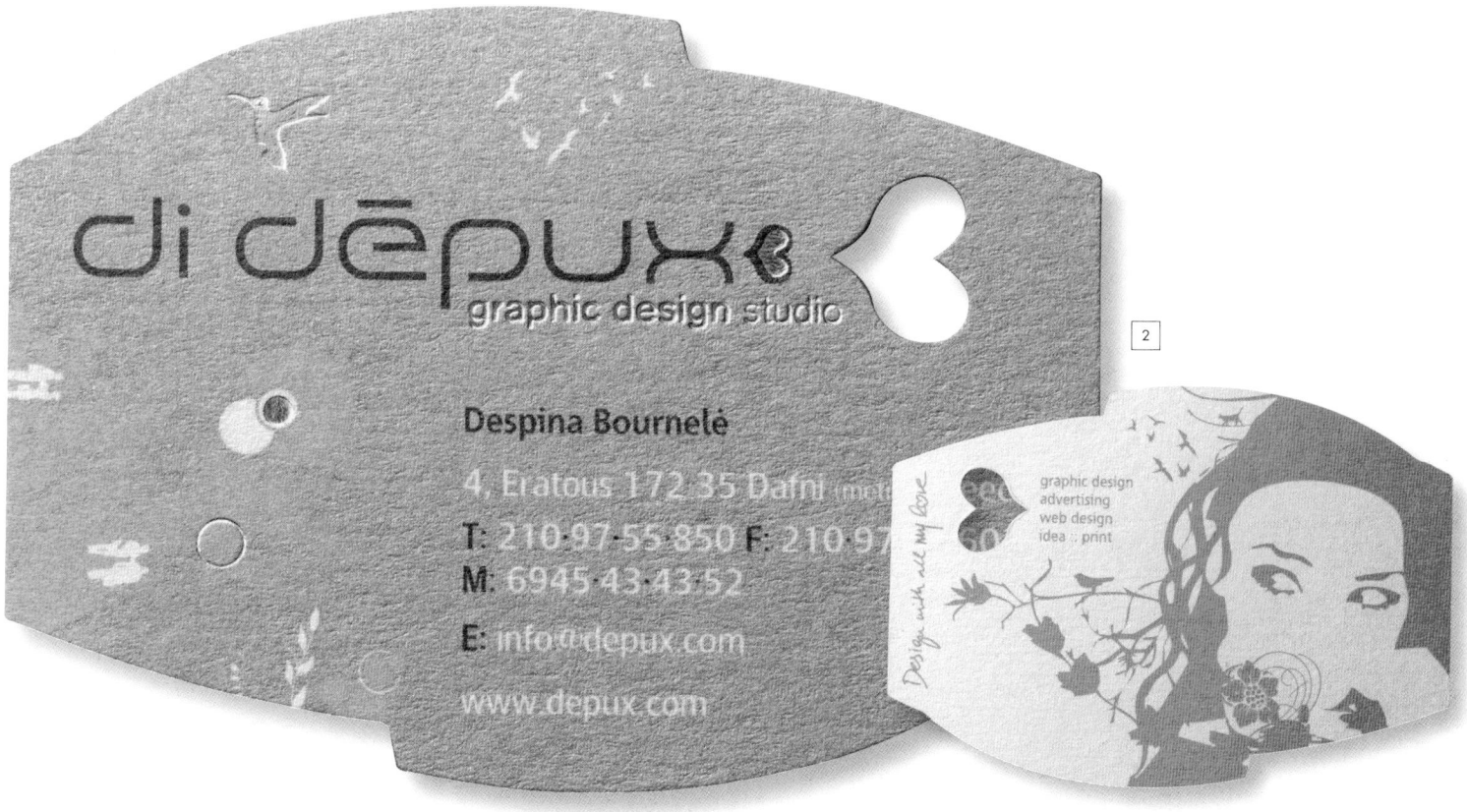
di dēpux
graphic design studio
Despina Bournelē
4, Eratous 172 35 Dafni
T: 210·97·55·850 F: 210·97
M: 6945·43·43·52
E: info@depux.com
www.depux.com
Design with all my love
graphic design
advertising
web design
idea :: print

2

3

ΚΑΤΕΡΙΝΑ ΒΕΝΙΟΥ
ΔΙΑΚΟΣΜΗΤΡΙΑ

mob. 6944.91.99.48

de:tales:
DESIGN STORIES

4

1

design firm: Di Depux
art director: Despina Bournele
designer: Despina Bournele
client: Ioannis Ragavas
software/hardware: Adobe Illustrator CS
paper/materials: CMYK, Velvet 350 grade

2

design firm: Di Depux
art director: Despina Bournele
designer: Despina Bournele
client: Di Depux
software/hardware: Adobe Illustrator CS
paper/materials: 2 Pantone, Curious Metallics A067, 250 grade

3

design firm: Di Depux
art director: Despina Bournele
designer: Despina Bournele
client: Katerina Veniou, Eleni Akermanoglou
software/hardware: Adobe Illustrator CS
paper/materials: CMYK, Velvet 350 grade

4

design firm: Di Depux
art director: Despina Bournele
designer: Despina Bournele
client: Dora
software/hardware: Adobe Illustrator CS
paper/materials: CMYK, Velvet 350 grade

TROY VERRETT, CSI, CDT
principal
tv@insitedevelopments.com
504.610.7238 CELL
Insite Developments, LLC
Building 11935, Suite 3
N.E. Nineteenth Drive
North Miami FL 33181
954.854.4312 TEL
504.412.9796 FAX
WWW.INSITEDEVELOPMENTS.COM
architectural services
real estate development
planning
NEW ORLEANS | MIAMI
WWW.INSITEDEVELOPMENTS.COM
architectural services
real estate development
planning
TROY VERRETT, CSI, CDT
principal
tv@insitedevelopments.com
504.610.7238 CELL
Insite Developments, LLC
822 Perdido Street
Suite 101
New Orleans LA 70112
504.412.9797 TEL
504.412.9796 FAX
in|site

1

ANGARA
ANKUR DAGA
CHIEF EXECUTIVE OFFICER
15 WEST 47TH STREET, SUITE 1303, NEW YORK, NY 10036
TEL. 877 9 ANGARA FAX. 201 503 8159 WWW.ANGARA.COM
CELL. 646 705 3999 ANKUR.DAGA@ANGARA.COM

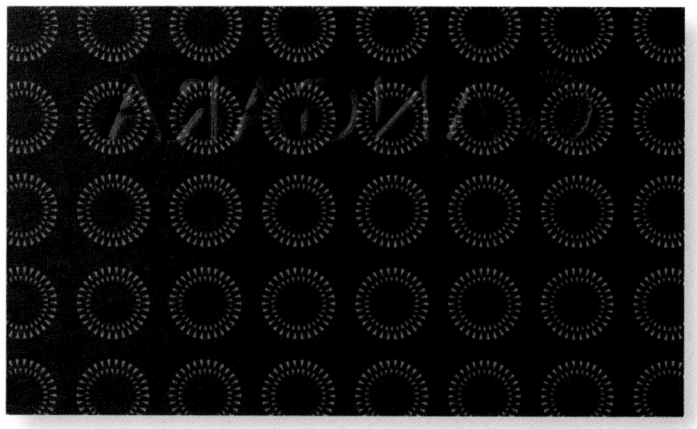

2

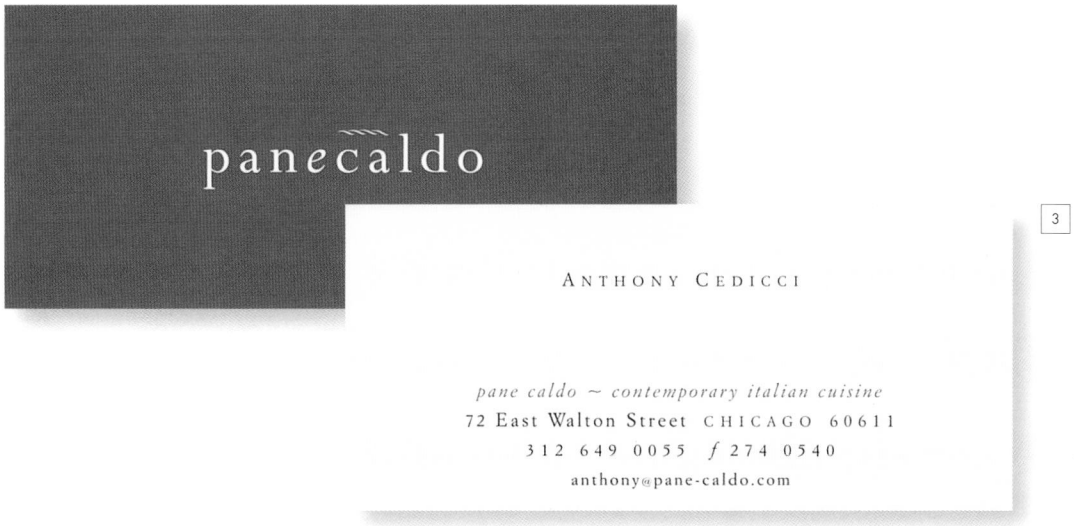

3

4

1

design firm: Zande + Newman Design
art director: Adam Newman
designer: Adam Newman
client: In Site Developments
software/hardware: Adobe Illustrator
paper/materials: Mohawk Superfine

2

design firm: Helena Seo Design
art director: Helena Seo
designer: Helena Seo
client: Angara, Inc.
software/hardware: Adobe Illustrator

3

design firm: Pagliuco Design Company
art director: Michael Pagliuco
designer: Michael Pagliuco
client: Pane Caldo
paper/materials: Strathmore

4

design firm: Lolight Design
art director: Aaron Deckler
designer: Aaron Deckler
client: Lolight Design
software/hardware: Adobe Illustrator and InDesign
paper/materials: Gilbert Esse White Green
printing: Offset printing 2/2

1

Lisa Evano
Account Supervisor
lisa@
counterpartCD.com
counterpartCD.com
901 323-4900 T
578-7878 F
40 South Idlewild Memphis TN 38104
THE VOICE OF THE BRAND
THE EAR OF THE CUSTOMER
communication +
COUNTERPART
design

PNL Pour se comprendre
PNL
Paul Mercier
Conseiller / enseignant
Centre de formation en Programmation Neuro Linguistique
C.P. 79158 / Gatineau (Qc) / J8Y 6V2 / centreformationpnl.com
t 819 770-5117 / f 819 777-6333 pmercier@centreformationpnl.com

2

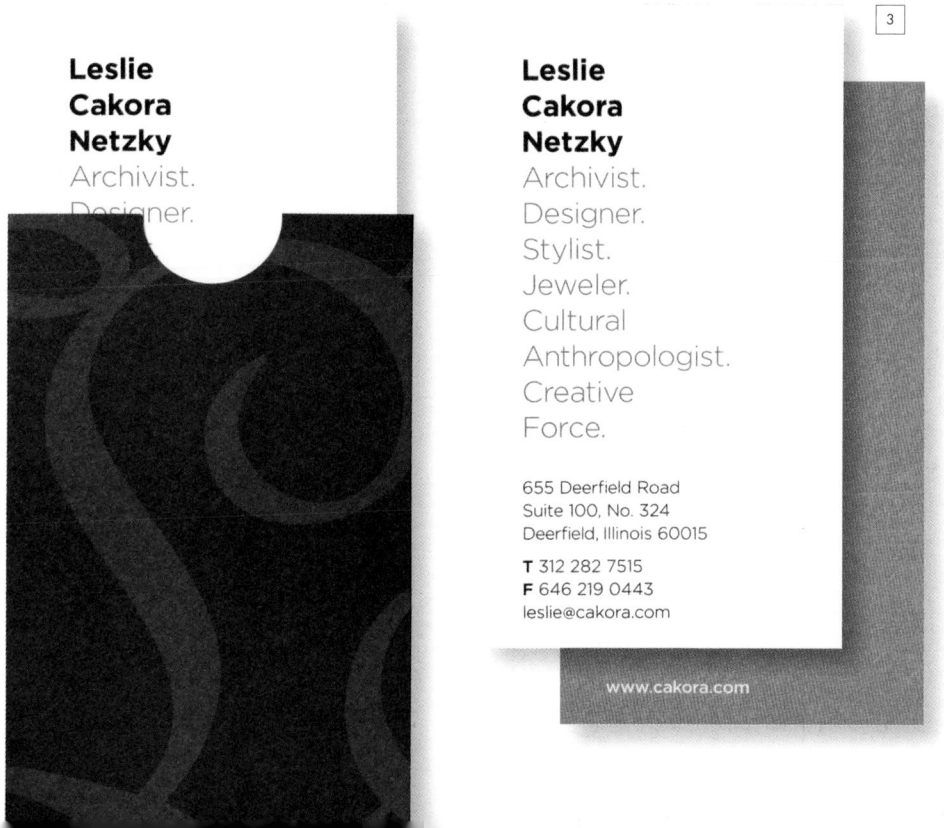
Leslie
Cakora
Netzky
Archivist.
Designer.
Leslie
Cakora
Netzky
Archivist.
Designer.
Stylist.
Jeweler.
Cultural
Anthropologist.
Creative
Force.
655 Deerfield Road
Suite 100, No. 324
Deerfield, Illinois 60015
T 312 282 7515
F 646 219 0443
leslie@cakora.com
www.cakora.com

3

1

948 SOUTH COOPER
MEMPHIS TN 38104
ph: 901.276.0002
dishmemphis.com

dish

dish

dish

CHRIS GARCIA
ph: 901.497.0463
chris@dishmemphis.com

BAR MANAGER

DEEJAY

GENERAL MANAGER

2

HONEY inspired american dining

42 Shewell Avenue Doylestown, Pennsylvania 18901

Joe & Amy McAtee, Proprietors CELL 215.230.9936

BUCKS COUNTY

HONEY

3

4

1

design firm: Switch Creative
art director: Michael Carpenter
designer: Michael Carpenter
client: SmartCity
software/hardware: Adobe Illustrator
paper/materials: Silk finish

2

design firm: Johnston Duffy
art director: Martin Duffy
designer: Andy Evans and Martin Duffy
client: Honey Restaurant
software/hardware: Adobe Illustrator and Photoshop on MAC
paper/materials: Mohawk Superfine

3

design firm: Chris Rooney Illustration/Design
designer: Chris Rooney
illustrator: Chris Rooney
client: Chris Rooney
software/hardware: Adobe Illustrator
paper/materials: 15 pt Tango C1S

4

design firm: A3 Design
art director: Amanda Altman
designer: Alan Altman
client: Hot Saké
software/hardware: Adobe Illustrator

BREWED IN
COLUMBUS, OHIO
USBREWING.COM
Est 1988
Est 1988
Est 1988
Columbus
BREWING COMPANY
GARY ROBINETTE HEAD BREWER
535 Short Street Columbus, Ohio 43215 gsrobinette@columbusbrewing.com
Brewery 614.224.3626 www.columbusbrewing.com

1

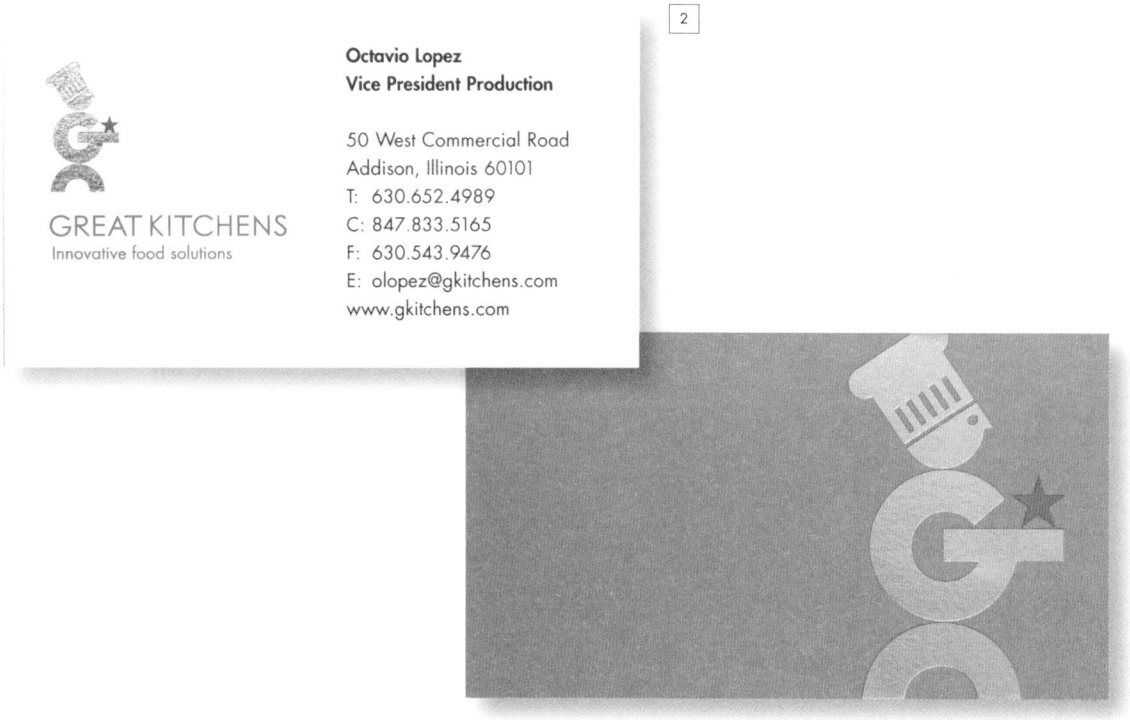
GREAT KITCHENS
Innovative food solutions
Octavio Lopez
Vice President Production
50 West Commercial Road
Addison, Illinois 60101
T: 630.652.4989
C: 847.833.5165
F: 630.543.9476
E: olopez@gkitchens.com
www.gkitchens.com

2

3

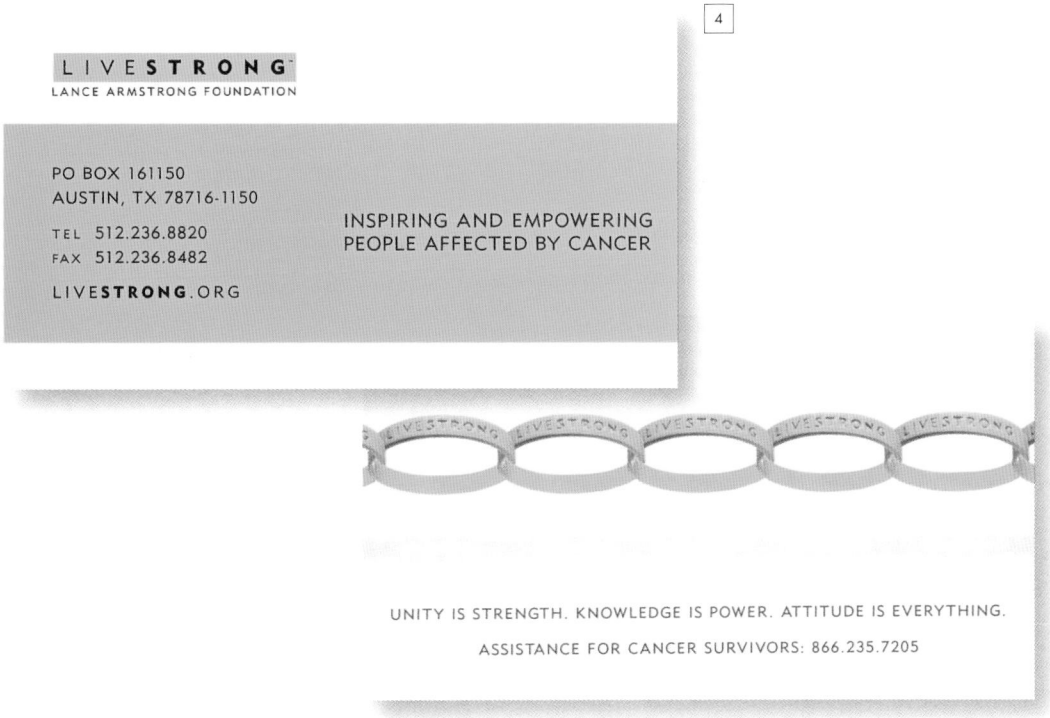

4

1

design firm: Element
art director: John McCollum
designer: Jeremy Slagle
client: Element
software/hardware: Adobe Illustrator and InDesign

2

design firm: Hartford Design
art director: Tim Hartford
designer: Scott Hight
client: Great Kitchens
software/hardware: Adobe Illustrator and InDesign CS

3

design firm: Thielen Designs
art director: Tony Thielen
designer: Tony Thielen
client: Thielen Designs
software/hardware: Adobe Illustrator
paper/materials: Classic Crest Natural 103 DTC, letterpress, Cougar 80 lb cover, eyelets, XL clothing stickers, price tags

4

design firm: Lance Armstrong Foundation in-house design
art director: Diana Guentzel
designer: Diana Guentzel
client: Lance Armstrong Foundation
software/hardware: Adobe Illustrator and Photoshop, and Quark Xpress
paper/materials: Classic Crest Solar White Smooth 110 lb cover

léboyé
www.leboyedesign.com
Jl Kemang Selatan 99a
Jakarta 12730 Indonesia
t 6221 7199676
f 6221 7199677
tanzil@leboyedesign.com
HERMAWAN TANZIL
creative director

1

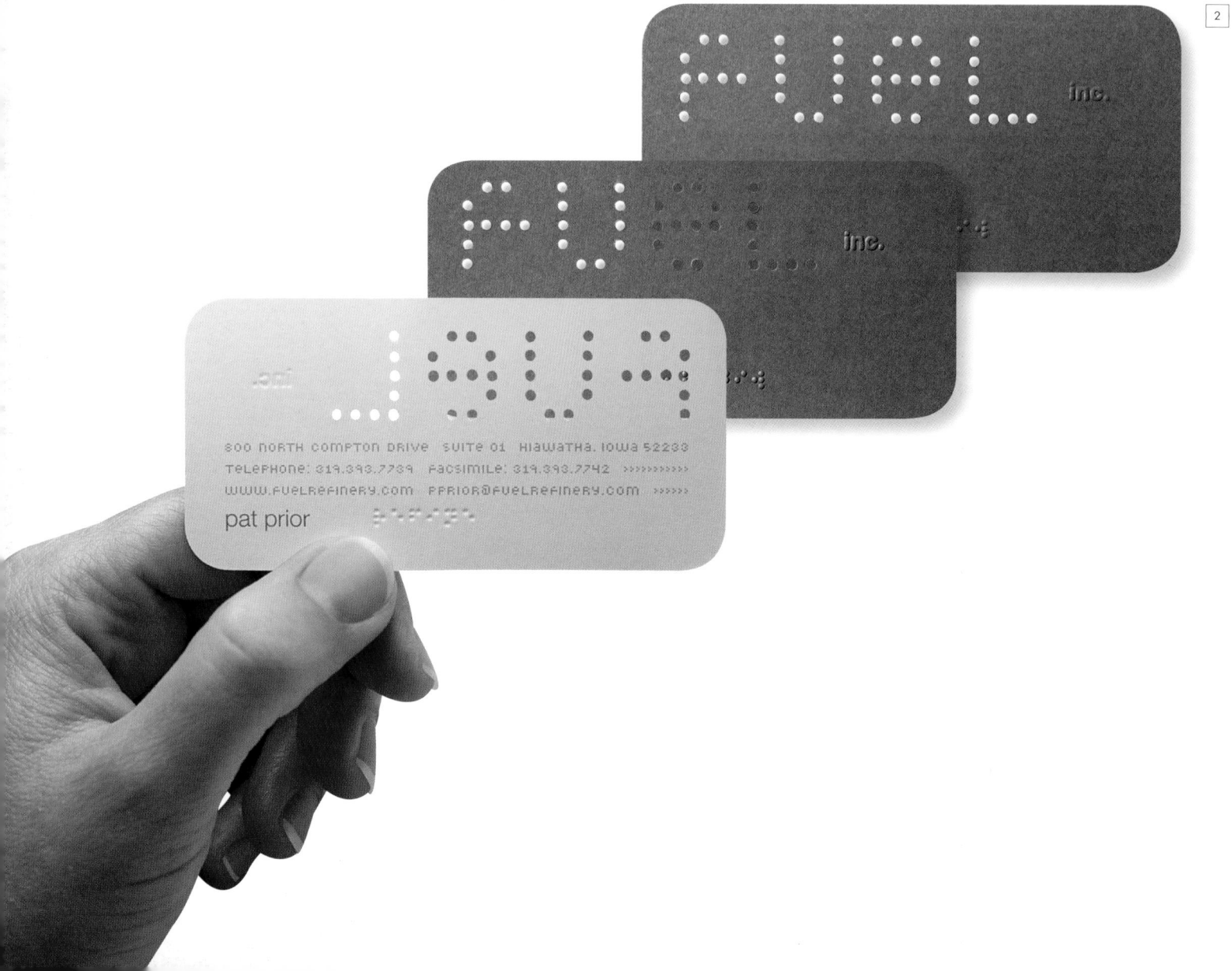
inc.
inc.
800 NORTH COMPTON DRIVE SUITE 01 HIAWATHA, IOWA 52233
TELEPHONE: 319.393.7739 FACSIMILE: 319.393.7742
WWW.FUELREFINERY.COM PPRIOR@FUELREFINERY.COM
pat prior

2

3

3 THINGS YOU SHOULD KNOW ABOUT MELISSA:

She has castrated a goat.
She is fluent in Pig Latin.
She kind of likes beets.

STRATEGY / ADVERTISING / DESIGN

MELISSA GEORGE
Production Manager

8220 LA MIRADA, SUITE 500
ALBUQUERQUE, NM 87109
email: mgeorge@whois3.com
phone: 505.293.2333
fax: 505.293.1198

4

MIKE EATON
Senior Art Director

13 Water Street, Holliston, MA 01746
V 508-429-0755 x18
F 508-429-0766
W www.m-d-g.com
E meaton@m-d-g.com

INC

1

design firm: LeBoYe
art director: Ignatius Hermawan Tanzil
designer: Ignatius Hermawan Tanzil and Ismiaji Cahyono
client: LeBoYe
software/hardware: Freehand MX
paper/materials: Curious 120 gsm and Conqueror Wove 250 gsm

2

design firm: Fuel
designer: Bill Bollman and Brian Cox
client: Fuel
software/hardware: Adobe Illustrator
paper/materials: Mohawk Superfine

3

design firm: 3
art director: Sam Maclay
designer: Tim McGrath
illustrator: Tim McGrath
client: 3
software/hardware: Quark Xpress and Adobe Illustrator
paper/materials: French Paper, gummed labels

4

design firm: MDG
art director: Mike Eaton
designer: Tim Merry (Creative Director
client: MDG
software/hardware: Adobe Illustrator - MAC
paper/materials: Monadnock Astrolite Smooth 200 lb cover, laser cut, debossed, and die-cut. 3-colo front. 1 color flood reverse.

1

2

1

design firm: Cinquino + Co.
art director: Ania J. Murray
designer: Ania J. Murray
client: Cinquino + Co.
software/hardware: Adobe Illustrator and InDesign
paper/materials: Embossed logo

2

design firm: Evenson Design
art director: Stan Evenson
designer: Mark Sojka
client: Mogomedia
software/hardware: EPS

3

design firm: MINE™
art director: Christopher Simmons
designer: Christopher Simmons
client: Steel Media
software/hardware: Adobe Illustrator CS2, Adobe InDesign CS2
paper/materials: Finch Bright White Smooth 130 lb cover, Fasson Softcream 70 lb

3

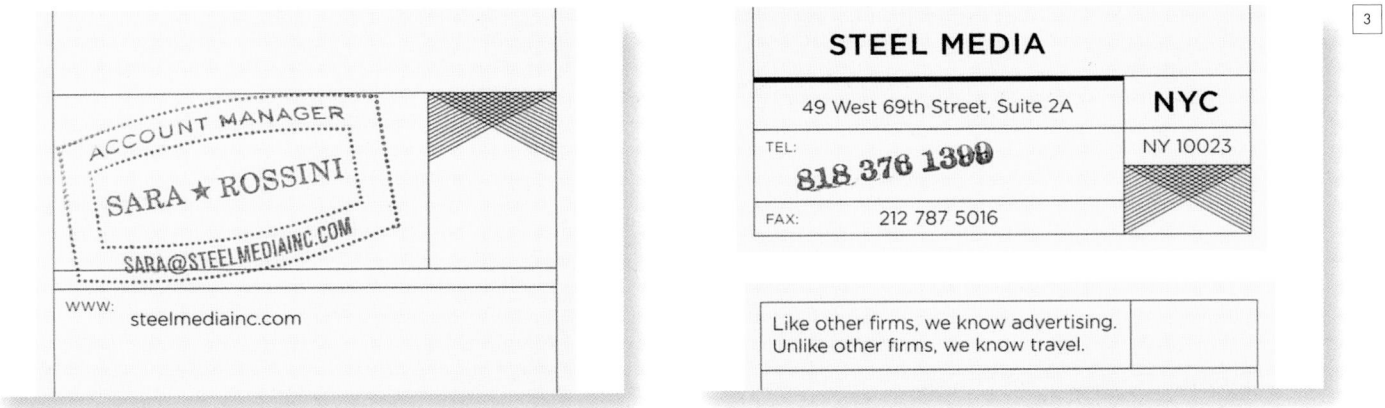
ACCOUNT MANAGER
SARA ★ ROSSINI
SARA@STEELMEDIAINC.COM
WWW:
steelmediainc.com
STEEL MEDIA
49 West 69th Street, Suite 2A
NYC
NY 10023
TEL:
818 376 1399
FAX:
212 787 5016
Like other firms, we know advertising.
Unlike other firms, we know travel.

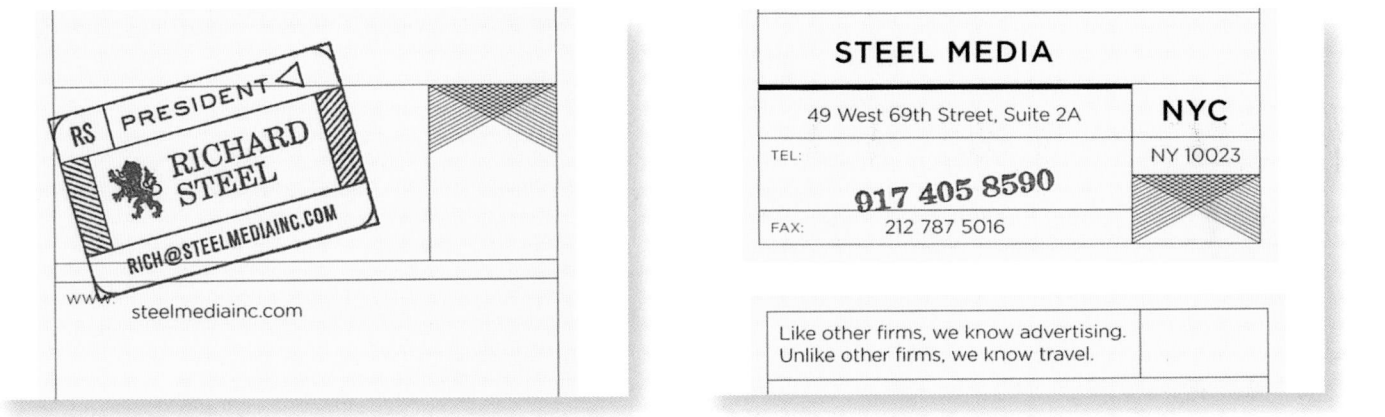
RS
PRESIDENT
RICHARD
STEEL
RICH@STEELMEDIAINC.COM
WWW:
steelmediainc.com
STEEL MEDIA
49 West 69th Street, Suite 2A
NYC
NY 10023
TEL:
917 405 8590
FAX:
212 787 5016
Like other firms, we know advertising.
Unlike other firms, we know travel.

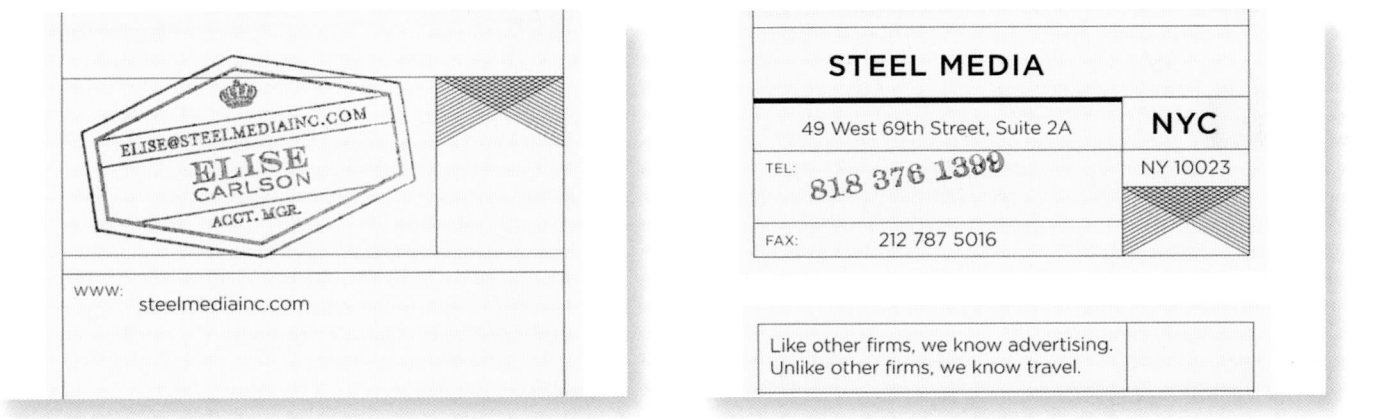
ELISE@STEELMEDIAINC.COM
ELISE
CARLSON
ACCT. MGR.
WWW:
steelmediainc.com
STEEL MEDIA
49 West 69th Street, Suite 2A
NYC
NY 10023
TEL:
818 376 1399
FAX:
212 787 5016
Like other firms, we know advertising.
Unlike other firms, we know travel.

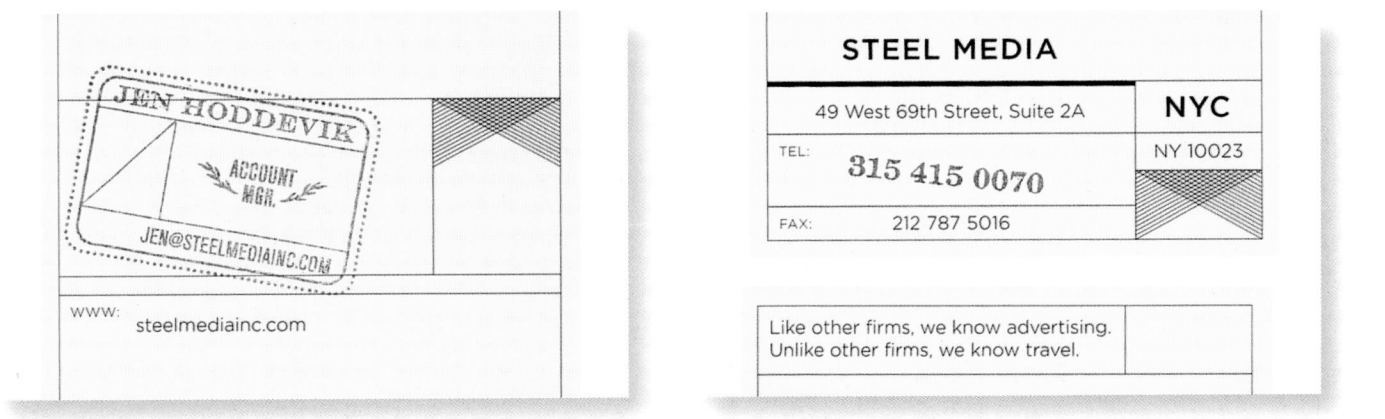
JEN HODDEVIK
ACCOUNT
MGR.
JEN@STEELMEDIAINC.COM
WWW:
steelmediainc.com
STEEL MEDIA
49 West 69th Street, Suite 2A
NYC
NY 10023
TEL:
315 415 0070
FAX:
212 787 5016
Like other firms, we know advertising.
Unlike other firms, we know travel.

evolutions

Berners Street
Soho Square
Oxford Street
Wells Street

Clare Buttress
Marketing Manager

T 020 7580 3333
M 07985 303 034
clare@evolutions.tv

www.evolutions.tv

1

evolutions

Berners Street
Soho Square
Oxford Street
Wells Street

Clare Buttress
Marketing Manager

T 020 7580 3333
M 07985 303 034
clare@evolutions.tv

www.evolutions.tv

evolutions

Berners Street
Soho Square
Oxford Street
Wells Street

Clare Buttress
Marketing Manager

T 020 7580 3333
M 07985 303 034
clare@evolutions.tv

www.evolutions.tv

evolutions

Berners Street
Soho Square
Oxford Street
Wells Street

Clare Buttress
Marketing Manager

T 020 7580 3333
M 07985 303 034
clare@evolutions.tv

www.evolutions.tv

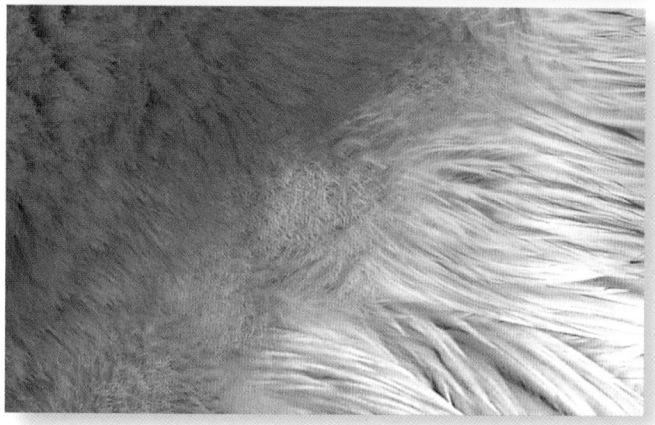

DUBLIN : LONDON : MANCHESTER
5 Schoolhouse Lane, Dublin 2, Ireland.
T: +353 (0)1 663 6400 **F**: +353 (0)1 663 6401

WWW.HKRARCHITECTS.COM

D: +353 (0)1 663 6480
M: +353 (0)87 691 1915
E: cgraefe@hkrarchitects.com

HKR ARCHITECTS

2

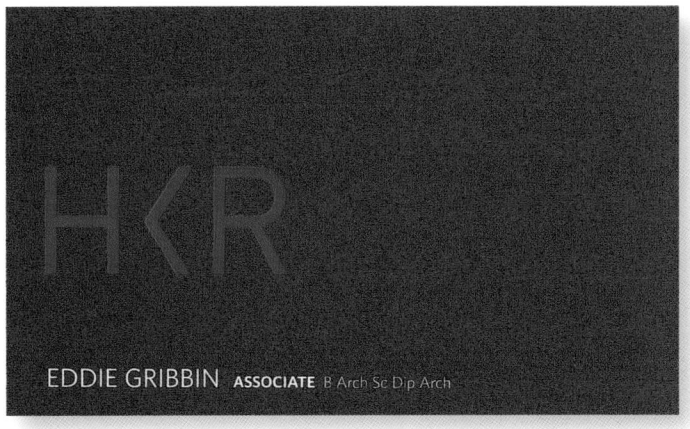

3

1

design firm: Salterbaxter
client: Evolutions
software/hardware: Tiff

2

design firm: Detail Design Studio
art director: Detail Design Studio
designer: Detail Design Studio
client: HKR Architects
software/hardware: Adobe Illustrator and Quark Xpress
paper/materials: Arcoprint

3

design firm: David Clark Design
art director: David Clark
designer: Becky Gelder
client: Amatucci Photography
software/hardware: Adobe Illustrator CS
paper/materials: Touche Black cover, Fasson Crack and Peel
printing: Western Printing

XANTHE matychak
ehtnax@yahoo.com > 607 342 2269

1

THOMAS
WOOD PRODUCTS
WILLIAM E. THOMAS
(610)777-6352
174 BRAN ROAD, SINKING SPRING, PENNSYLVANIA
POINTED STAKES, LUMBER, SEASONED FIREWOOD, CUSTOM SAWING
(mail) 33 S. 24th St. Mt. Penn, PA 19606

2

3

MOREBARN

{ARTIST & PRODUCER MANAGEMENT}

GARY WALDMAN | 212.777.0611

GARY@MOREBARN.COM

628 BROADWAY SUITE 502

NEW YORK / NEW YORK / 10012

"I ONCE WENT DOWN TO NEIL YOUNG'S RANCH
AND HE ROWED ME OUT INTO THE MIDDLE OF A LAKE
(PUTTING MY LIFE IN HIS HANDS ONCE AGAIN).
He waved at someone invisible
and music started to play, in the countryside.
I REALIZED NEIL HAD HIS HOUSE WIRED AS THE LEFT SPEAKER,
AND HIS BARN WIRED AS THE RIGHT SPEAKER.
And Elliot Mazer, his engineer, said 'How is it?'
AND NEIL SHOUTED BACK: 'MORE BARN!'"
– GRAHAM NASH

4

GRASSCUTTERS

Arnie & Treston Clark
2 Walker Road
Kennebunk, Maine

985-3167 229-6924 294-1034

1

design firm: The Human Race
art director: Xanthe Matychak
designer: Xanthe Matychak
client: Xanthe Matychak
software/hardware: Adobe InDesign
paper/materials: Rubber stamp, reused paperboard packaging

2

design firm: Johnston Duffy
art director: Martin Duffy
designer: Martin Duffy
client: Thomas Wood Company
software/hardware: Adobe Illustrator and Photos
paper/materials: Wood Veneer

3

design firm: Nothing: Something: NY
art director: Kevin Landwehr
designer: Kevin Landwehr and Devin Becker
client: Morebarn Artist and Producer Management

4

design firm: Boxwood Press
art director: Cheryl L. Clark
designer: Cheryl L. Clark
client: Grasscutters
paper/materials: Colored STAPLES stock

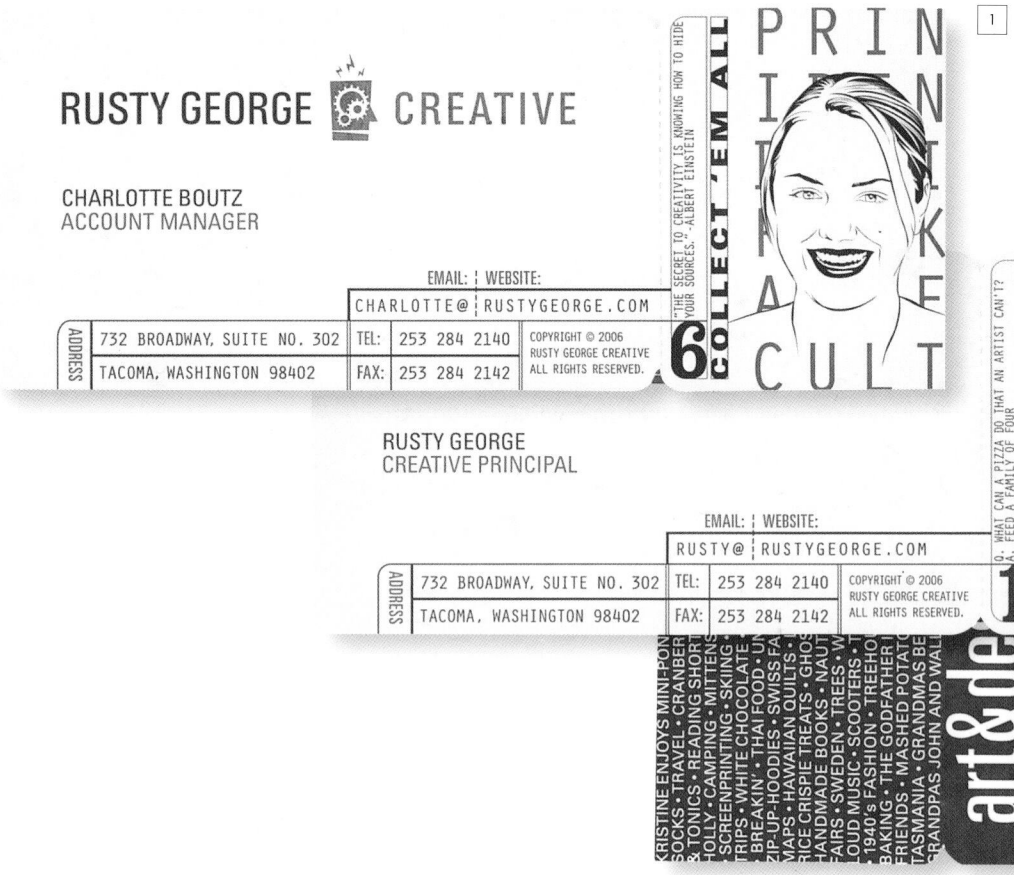
RUSTY GEORGE CREATIVE
CHARLOTTE BOUTZ
ACCOUNT MANAGER
EMAIL: | WEBSITE:
CHARLOTTE@ | RUSTYGEORGE.COM
ADDRESS
732 BROADWAY, SUITE NO. 302
TACOMA, WASHINGTON 98402
TEL: 253 284 2140
FAX: 253 284 2142
COPYRIGHT © 2006
RUSTY GEORGE CREATIVE
ALL RIGHTS RESERVED.
"THE SECRET TO CREATIVITY IS KNOWING HOW TO HIDE YOUR SOURCES." -ALBERT EINSTEIN
6
COLLECT 'EM ALL
RUSTY GEORGE
CREATIVE PRINCIPAL
EMAIL: | WEBSITE:
RUSTY@ | RUSTYGEORGE.COM
ADDRESS
732 BROADWAY, SUITE NO. 302
TACOMA, WASHINGTON 98402
TEL: 253 284 2140
FAX: 253 284 2142
COPYRIGHT © 2006
RUSTY GEORGE CREATIVE
ALL RIGHTS RESERVED.
Q. WHAT CAN A PIZZA DO THAT AN ARTIST CAN'T?
A. FEED A FAMILY OF FOUR
1
COLLECT 'EM ALL
art&de
DIGITAL
PACKAGING
ADVERTISIN
CULTURE

1

David Bishop
Creative Director
FRONT MEDIA
richard@frontmedia.co.uk
www.frontmedia.co.uk
+44 (0)1621 890 220
+44 (0)7880 743 235

2

3

MATHIAS SCHAAB, Dipl.-Kfm. Medienwirtschaft

WEBRAUM

Agentur für interaktive Medien, Rosenthaler Str. 39, 10178 Berlin
Office 030 63 37 11 87, Fax 030 63 37 11 88, Mobil 0163 718 41 75
E-Mail schaab@webraum.de, Internet www.webraum.de

4

CALARUS GROUP
Valuable. Strategic. Solutions.

Naila Mall-Goodro, M.A.
PRESIDENT

19141 Stone Oak Parkway
Suite 104 #248
San Antonio, Texas 78258
T/F 830 438 5012
M 619 985 9932

ngoodro@calarusgroup.com
www.calarusgroup.com

CALARUS GROUP
VALUABLE. STRATEGIC. SOLUTIONS.

19141 Stone Oak Parkway
Suite 104 #248
San Antonio, Texas 78258
T/F 830 438 5012

www.calarusgroup.com

1

design firm: Rusty George Creative
art director: Rusty George
designer: Lance Kagey
client: Rusty George Creative
software/hardware: Adobe Illustrator
paper/materials: French Paper, Durotone Butcher Blue

2

design firm: Frontmedia
art director: Neil Maidment and David Bishop
designer: Neil Maidment
client: Frontmedia
software/hardware: Adobe Illustrator and InDesign
paper/materials: Arctic Munken Lynx

3

design firm: R975
art director: Marcel Kummerer
designer: Marcel Kummerer
client: Webraum

4

design firm: Murillo Design, Inc.
art director: Roland Murillo
designer: Roland Murillo
client: Calarus Group
paper/materials: Strathmore Ultimate White 100 lb cover

1

DEFINING BUSINESS. BY DESIGN.™

MILESDESIGN
ERIC FOLZENLOGEL
eric@milesdesign.com
tel 317.915.8693 | cell 317.919.0642 | www.milesdesign.com
5170 East 65th Street, Indianapolis, IN 46220

2

ZANDE+NEWMAN DESIGN
902 Jefferson Ave. Nº 1
New Orleans LA 70115
504.891.4526 tel
504.891.3919 fax

3

DesignRe
Email.
info@designreligion.co.uk

eligion.
DesignReligion.
Hampton Court
Rainbow Hill
Worcester WR3 8NF
Telephone.
+44 (0)1905 724 707
Mobile.
+44 (0)7977 107 663
Facsimile.
+44 (0)1905 724 768
www.
designreligion.co.uk

DesignRe
Tim Corbyn
Senior Creative
Email.
tim@designreligion.co.uk

eligion.
DesignReligion.
Hampton Court
Rainbow Hill
Worcester WR3 8NF
Telephone.
+44 (0)1905 724 707
Mobile.
+44 (0)7789 005 856
Facsimile.
+44 (0)1905 724 768
www.
designreligion.co.uk

1

ANDREW JENKINSON
CREATIVE DIRECTOR / CO-FOUNDER
+44 (0) 7739 981 842 ANDREW@FOLK.UK.COM

Folk

FOLK CREATIVE MARKETING 2A LUKE STREET LONDON EC2A 4NT
T +44 (0) 207 739 8444 F +44 (0) 207 033 0018 W WWW.FOLK.UK.COM

MATT BUTTERWORTH
MANAGING DIRECTOR / CO-FOUNDER
+44 (0) 7740 738 556 MATT@FOLK.UK.COM

Folk

FOLK CREATIVE MARKETING 2A LUKE STREET LONDON EC2A 4NT
T +44 (0) 207 739 8444 F +44 (0) 207 033 0018 W WWW.FOLK.UK.COM

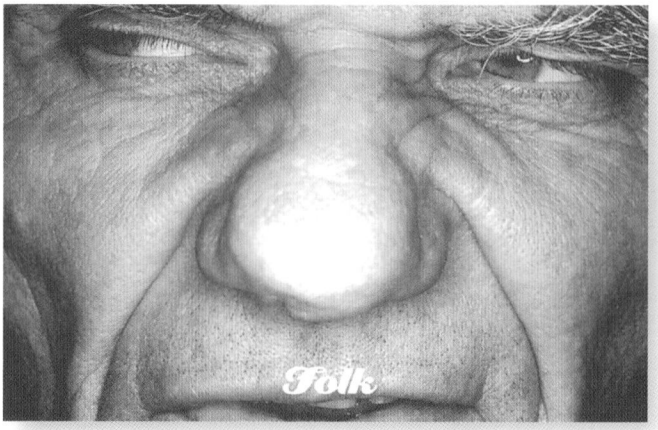

2

3

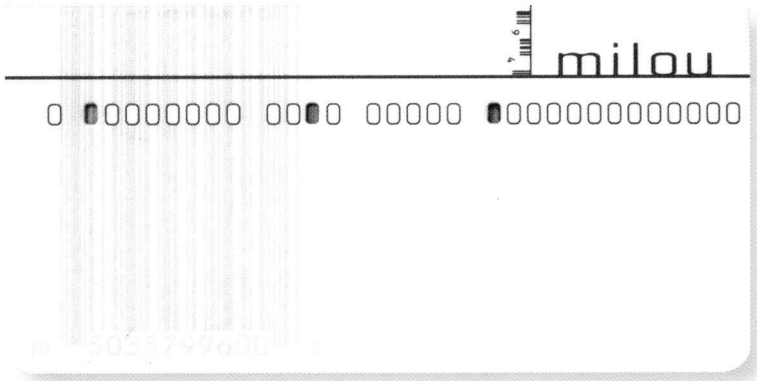

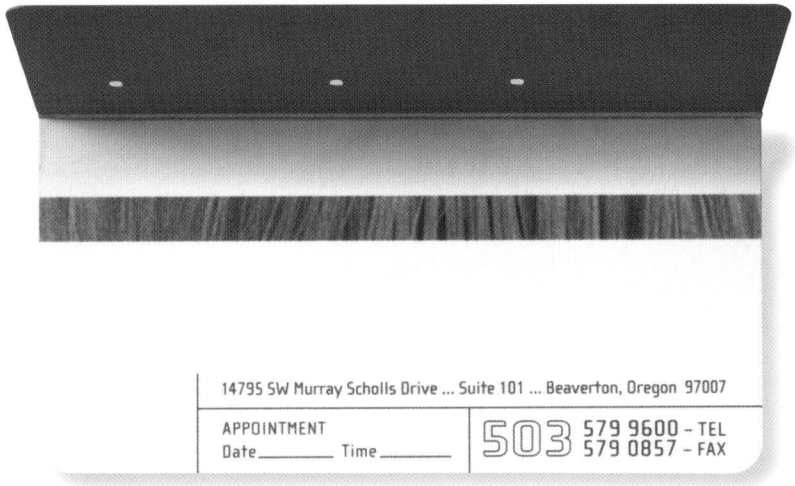

4

1

design firm: Folk Creative Ltd.
art director: Andrew Jenkinson
designer: Andrew Jenkinson
client: Folk Creative Ltd.
software/hardware: Adobe InDesign and Photoshop
paper/materials: Uncoated 2-color Litho

2

design firm: Fangman Design
art director: Matt Fangman
designer: Matt Fangman
illustrator: Matt Fangman
client: Fangman Design
software/hardware: Adobe Illustrator
paper/materials: French Paper Durotone, Butcher White 100 lb cover

3

design firm: Dotzero Design
designer: Karen Wippich and Jon Wippich
client: Davis Agency
software/hardware: Adobe Illustrator and Photoshop
paper/materials: Classic Crest

4

design firm: Miles Design
art director: Josh Miles
designer: Eric Folzenlogel
client: T-Box
software/hardware: Adobe Illustrator CS
paper/materials: Cougar White 100 lb

1

ONEMETHOD
Patricia Tay Account Executive
7145 West Credit Ave, Building 1, Suite 102
Mississauga, Ontario L5N 6J7 Canada
T 905 603 0180 EXT.800 F 905 603 8180
C 416 993 7660 patricia@onemethod.com
www.onemethod.com

2

林赛 卡姆
创始人，副总裁
别忘了联络：
电话 415 454 7844
传真 415 454 7834
电子邮件 LINDSAY@NAGTAGS.COM
通讯地址 PO BOX 1058 LARKSPUR, CA 94977
nt
NAGTAGS

lindsay kamm!
don't forget to:
call 415 454 7844
fax 415 454 7834
email LINDSAY@NAGTAGS.COM
write PO BOX 1058 LARKSPUR, CA 94977
nt
NAGTAGS

1

design firm: Onemethod Inc.
art director: Amin Todai
designer: Ryan Saley
client: Onemethod Inc.
software/hardware: Adobe Illustrator
paper/materials: Centura

2

design firm: MINE™
art director: Christopher Simmons
designer: Christopher Simmons and Kate Earhart
client: Nagtags
software/hardware: Adobe Illustrator CS2, Adobe InDesign CS2
paper/materials: Mohawk Superfine Ultrawhite Smooth 130 lb DTC

3

design firm: Element
art director: Megan Graham
designer: Megan Graham
client: Vocal Consulting Group
software/hardware: Adobe InDesign

4

design firm: Turnstyle
art director: Ben Graham, Steve Watson

1

pak mei yaolin kung fu school
白眉吳館友聯龍獅團
ken wu |
吳建強
chief instructor
+61 416 241 975
kenwu@yaolin.com.au
www.yaolin.com.au

Tequila Mockingbird
Music & Sound Design
Jeremiah Clifton
Engineer/Webmaster
jeremiah@tequilamockingbird.com
Mobile: 512-757-3808
306 West Sixteenth Street
Austin, Texas 78701
Phone: 512-499-8655
Fax: 512-499-8057
tequilamockingbird.com

2

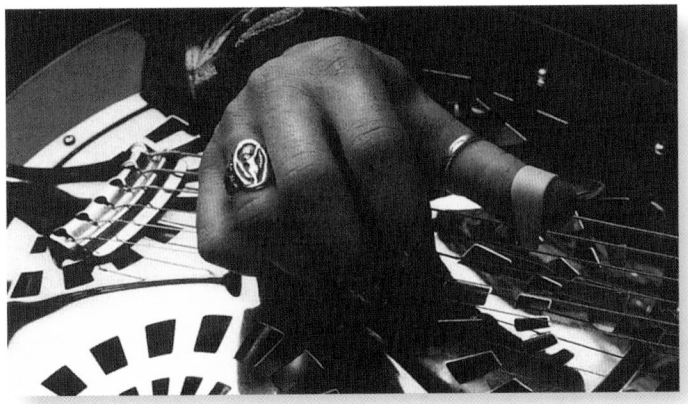

3

The
24 HR.
Plays
PHILIP NAUDÉ
philip@24hourplays.com
Cell: 917.892.8290
www.24hourplays.com

1

b:lok

BLOK DESIGN | VANESSA ARRIOJA | T: [52 55] 55 15 24 23

SOMBRERETE 515-1 CONDESA MEXICO DF 06170 | va@blokdesign.com

モダンダンス

MAIKO

2

3

4

1

design firm: Blok
art director: Vanessa Eckstein
designer: Vanessa Eckstein
client: Blok
software/hardware: Adobe Illustrator
paper/materials: Strathmore Ultimate White

2

design firm: Foda Studio
art director: Jett Butler
designer: Jett Butler
client: Maiko Japanese Restaurant
software/hardware: Adobe Illustrator
paper/materials: Neenah Classic Laid
Natural White 120 lb cover

3

design firm: Scott Adams Design Associates
designer: Scott Adams
client: Metropolitan Partners
software/hardware: Quark Xpress
paper/materials: Neenah Classic Crest

4

design firm: Campbell Fisher Design
art director: Greg Fisher
designer: Stacy Crawford
client: CDK Partners
software/hardware: Adobe Illustrator
paper/materials: Classic Crest 165 lb cover

ROOT
IDEA
KEN LEE
CREATIVE VEGETARIAN
FLAT 2304 PROGRESS COMMERCIAL BLDG
9 IRVING STREET CAUSEWAY BAY HK
T 29730056 * F 29730035 * M 97070066
WWW.ROOTIDEA.COM * KENLEE@ROOTIDEA.COM
意念根源
李錦雄
創作素食者
香港銅鑼灣伊榮街9號欣榮商業大廈2304室
電29730056 傳29730035 手機97070066
WWW.ROOTIDEA.COM KENLEE@ROOTIDEA.COM

1

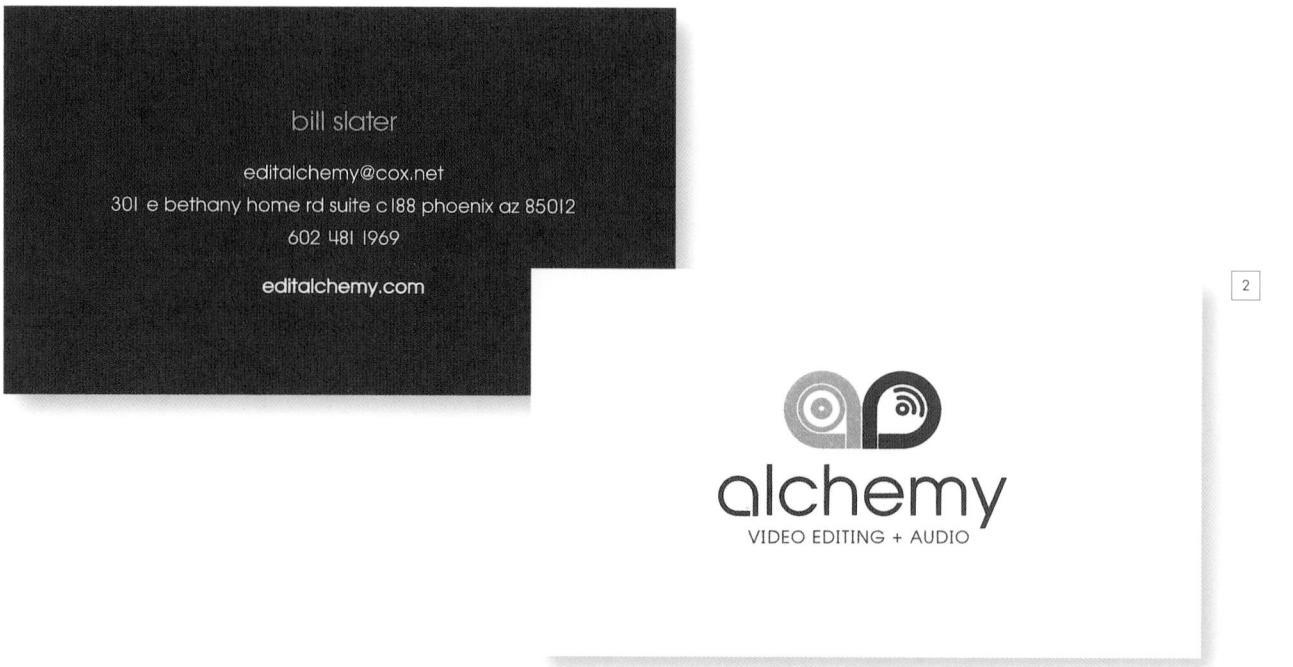
bill slater
editalchemy@cox.net
301 e bethany home rd suite c188 phoenix az 85012
602 481 1969
editalchemy.com
alchemy
VIDEO EDITING + AUDIO

2

3

4

1

design firm: Root Idea
art director: Ken Lee
designer: Ken Lee
client: Root Idea
software/hardware: Photoshop and Adobe Illustrator
paper/materials: Antalis, soft touch

2

design firm: Campbell Fisher Design
art director: Mike Campbell
designer: Stacy Crawford
client: Alchemy
software/hardware: Adobe Illustrator
paper/materials: Domtar Solutions
Cararra White 100 lb cover

3

design firm: dpd studio
art director: Dennis Purcell
designer: Dennis Purcell
client: dpd studio
software/hardware: Adobe Illustrator
paper/materials: French Paper Company
Smart White

4

design firm: dpd studio
art director: Dennis Purcell
designer: Dennis Purcell
client: JNR8
software/hardware: Adobe Illustrator

1

220 N. Zapata Hwy. #11
Laredo, TX 78043
U.S. phone 469-361-2309
kroark@zaragozavineyards.com
ZARAGOZA
VINEYARDS
KIRK ROARK
Aldama #3 C.P. 37700
San Miguel de Allende, GTO
mobile 044-415-100-3788
kroark@zaragozavineyards.com

2

GRAPHIC DESIGN
ADVERTISING
ILLUSTRATION
IDENTITY
WEB DESIGN
ENVIRONMENTAL
PACKAGING
TEXTILE
EVENTS
hautehauscreative
HAUTE HAU
creative

hahacreative.com
FOR SERIOUSLY COOL IDEAS
hautehauscreative
DON LEWIS
P.O.BOX 3352
AUSTIN, TEXAS 78764
PHONE:(512)477-7592
FAX:(512)477-5020
EMAIL:DON@HAHACREATIVE.COM

3

1

design firm: Sibley Peteet Design—Dallas
art director: Don Sibley
designer: Brandon Kirk
client: Zaragoza Vineyards
software/hardware: Adobe Illustrator

2

design firm: Haute Haus Creative
art director: Don Lewis
designer: Don Lewis
client: Haute Haus Creative
software/hardware: Freehand and Quark Xpress
paper/materials: Classic Crest, scored, glued

3

design firm: Archrival
art director: Joel Kreutzer
designer: Joel Kreutzer
client: Kopsa Otte
software/hardware: Adobe Illustrator CS2

4

4

design firm: Di Depux
art director: Despina Bournele
designer: Despina Bournele
client: Constantinos Delis and Demitra
software/hardware: Adobe Illustrator CS
paper/materials: 3 Pantone, Curious 250 gsm

1

Zita Lefebvre
*Director of Operations
zita.lefebvre@turner.com
300 North Third Street
Burbank, CA 91502
P (818) 729-4036
F (818) 729-4093
CARTOON NETWORK STUDIOS

TM and © 2006 Cartoon Network.

TM and © 2006 Cartoon Network.

Zita Lefebvre
*Director of Operations
zita.lefebvre@turner.com
300 North Third Street
Burbank, CA 91502
P (818) 729-4036
F (818) 729-4093
CARTOON NETWORK STUDIOS

Zita Lefebvre
*Director of Operations
zita.lefebvre@turner.com
300 North Third Street
Burbank, CA 91502
P (818) 729-4036
F (818) 729-4093
CARTOON NETWORK STUDIOS

TM and © 2006 Cartoon Network.

TM and © 2006 Cartoon Network.

Zita Lefebvre
*Director of Operations
zita.lefebvre@turner.com
300 North Third Street
Burbank, CA 91502
P (818) 729-4036
F (818) 729-4093
CARTOON NETWORK STUDIOS

2

3

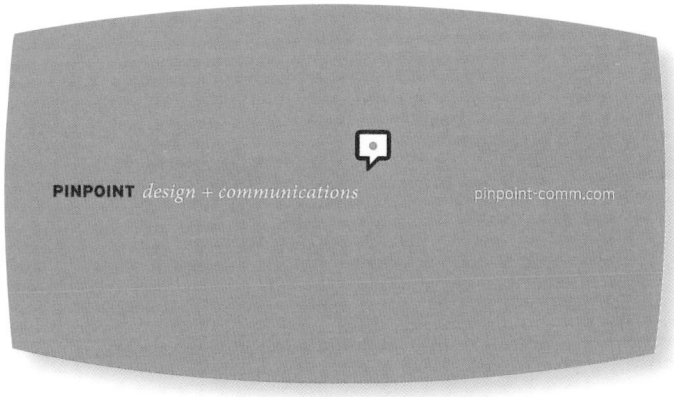

1

design firm: Trade Creative Services
art director: Jay Rogers

2

design firm: Joe Shouldice Design
art director: Joe Shouldice

3

design firm: Pinpoint Communications
art director: James Kluetz and Paul Cooper

1

Baseman Design Associates
221 Mather Road
Jenkintown, Pennsylvania 19046 **USA**

BDA

Frank Baseman
frank@basemandesign.com
www.basemandesign.com

t. 215 885 7157
f. 215 885 7156

2

JEFF BREAZEALE PARTNER

3116 MAIN STREET, DALLAS, TEXAS 75226
jeff@matchboxstudio.com

PHONE 214 939 3100
FAX 214 939 3400

3

FY2K
Modern Furniture
Collections

4 Foster Street Surry Hills NSW 2010
T +61 2 9281 1771 F +61 2 9281 1774
julie@fy2k.com.au
www.fy2k.com.au

Julie Angland

4

1

design firm: Baseman Design Associates
art director: Frank Baseman
designer: Frank Baseman
client: Baseman Design Associates
software/hardware: Quark Xpress
paper/materials: Crane's 130 lb cover
letterpress printing

2

design firm: The Matchbox Studio
art director: Jeff Breazeale and Liz Burnett
designer: Jeff Breazeale and Liz Burnett
client: The Matchbox Studio
paper/materials: Classic Cotton Bristol
Solar White cover

3

design firm: There
art director: There
designer: There
client: FY2K
software/hardware: Adobe Illustrator
paper/materials: Various

4

design firm: JSDS
art director: JSDS
designer: Justin Skeesuck
client: JSDS
software/hardware: Adobe Illustrator
paper/materials: Vintage postcard
letterpress

DESIGN AKERS
2810 Franklin Street
Apartment 10
San Francisco, CA
94123
415 928 8929
Kevin Akers

DESIGN AKERS

1

1441 EAST PENDER STREET, VANCOUVER
BRITISH COLUMBIA, V5L1V7 CANADA
FACSIMILE 604 669 2010 _ www.battersbyhowat.com
BETTINA BALCAEN
604 669 9647 _ bettina@battersbyhowat.com

2

BATTERSBY
HOWAT

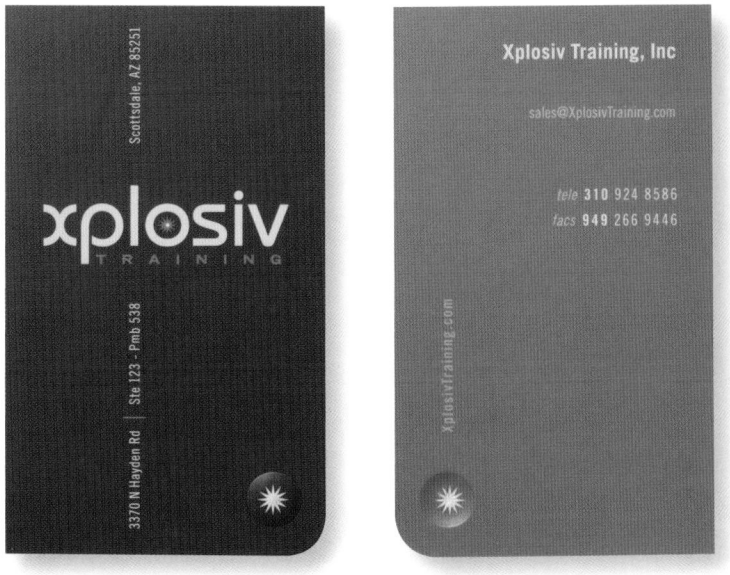

3

4

1

design firm: Kevin Akers Design and Imagery
art director: Kevin Akers
designer: Kevin Akers
illustrator: Kevin Akers
client: Kevin Akers
software/hardware: Adobe Illustrator
paper/materials: Simpson

2

design firm: Subplot Design, Inc.
art director: Roy White, Matthew Clark
designer: Steph Gibson
client: Battersbyhowat Architects
software/hardware: Adobe Illustrator
paper/materials: Curious Touch, Mohawk Superfine

3

design firm: Flipcide
art director: Roy Dequina
designer: Roy Dequina
client: Xplosiv Training
software/hardware: Adobe Illustrator
paper/materials: TopKote Uncoated 110 lb

4

design firm: Nothing: Something: NY
art director: Kevin Landwehr
designer: Kevin Landwehr and Devin Becker
client: Nothing: Something: NY
paper/materials: Neenah Classic Crest 130 lb

DANNI hang
* love-by-design.com
po box 1134
la habra, CA 90633
p: 562.773.0794
e: danni@love-by-design.com
love by
DESIGN

1

love by
DESIGN

1

EMIGRE FILM

N:52

RIO PANUCO 36, COL. CUAUHTEMOC, MEXICO DF, 06500

teléfono N:52 55 / 9150 7300 / 15 fernando@emigrefilm.com

EMIGRE FILM

2

SETH ROSENBERG

(917) 406 4212

INFO@SPEEDYFIXIT.COM

WWW.SPEEDYFIXIT.COM

INSURED | AVAILABLE 7 DAYS

NO JOB TOO SMALL

3

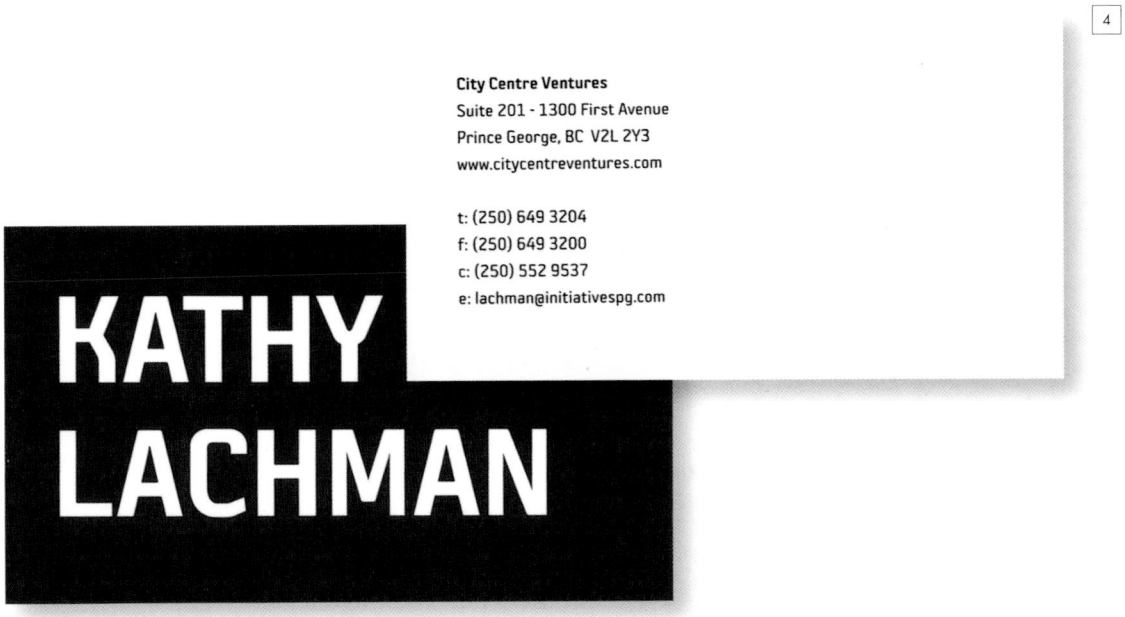

4

1

design firm: Blok
art director: Vanessa Eckstein
designer: Vanessa Eckstein, Mariana Contegni, Patricia Kleeberg
client: Émigré Film
software/hardware: Adobe Illustrator
paper/materials: Fox River Sirius Smooth

2

design firm: Matthew Schwartz Design Studio
art director: Matthew Schwartz
client: Speedy Fixit
software/hardware: Adobe Illustrator and InDesign

3

design firm: Nassar Design
art director: Nélida Nassar
designer: Nélida Nassar
client: Nassar Design
software/hardware: Quark Xpress
paper/materials: Curious Metallic Anodized, 1 color

4

design firm: smashLAB
art director: Eric Karjaluoto
designer: Javier Plug
illustrator: Javier Plug
client: City Centre Ventures
software/hardware: Adobe Illustrator
paper/materials: Save-A-Tree 100 lb cover

1

100% Funny Shirts.
Wear daily. Do not bleach.
Tumble dry low.
Made in the USA
SACK
www.sackwear.com
Shirts for people.
This business is located at
8220 La Mirada Place, Suite 500,
Albuquerque, New Mexico, 87109.
The phone number is 505.293.2333.
The email is info@sackwear.com.
SACK
www.sackwear.com
Shirts for people.
This business is located at
20 La Mirada Place, Suite 500,
uquerque, New Mexico, 87109.
hone number is 505.293.2333.
mail is info@sackwear.com.

2

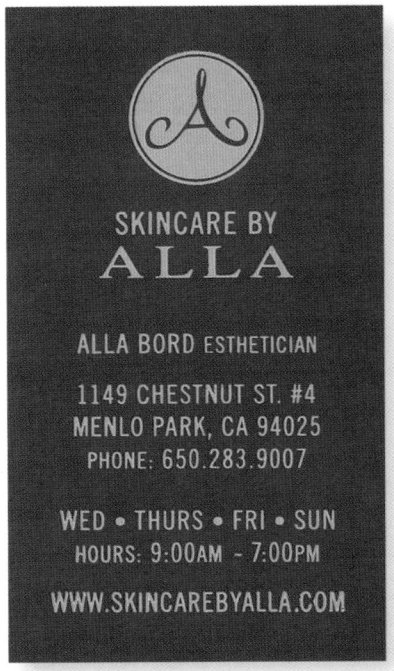

3

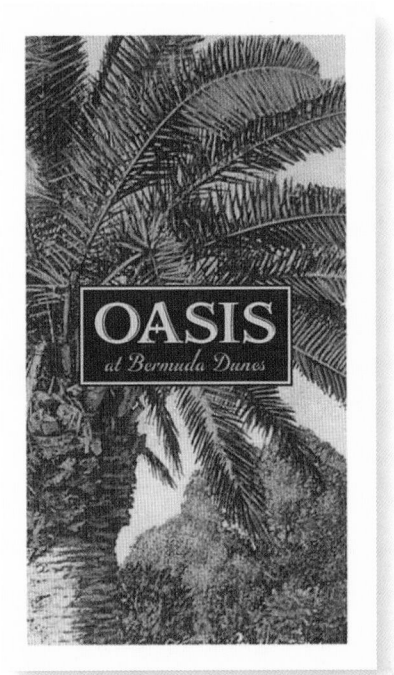

1

design firm: 3
art director: Sam Maclay
designer: Tim McGrath
illustrator: Tim McGrath
client: Sackwear.com
software/hardware: Quark Xpress and Adobe Illustrator
paper/materials: French Paper, with neck tags stitched in; Rubber stamps

2

design firm: Sandy Gin Design
designer: Sandy Gin
client: Skincare by Alla
software/hardware: Macromedia Freehand
paper/materials: Speckletone 100 lb cover, Foil Stamped

3

design firm: Dotzero Design
designer: Karen Wippich and Jon Wippich
client: Davis Agency
paper/materials: Classic Crest Natural White

1

THE GLOBAL LEGAL PLATFORM
www.serengetilaw.com

SERENGETI

GREG SHRIBER
Project Manager

T +1.425.748.5115
F +1.425.748.5116
E greg.shriber@serengetilaw.com

2018 156th Ave. NE
Suite No. 100
Bellevue, WA 98007

2

AMY JENKINS
amy@stickirice.com

sticki rice

1222 EAST BLVD
CHARLOTTE NC 28203
(p) 704.644.5363 (f) 704.248.8487

GIFTS | ACCENTS | HOME DECOR

sticki rice

WWW.STICKIRICE.COM

3

PERBACCO
ristorante + bar

www.perbaccosf.com

230 California Street
San Francisco, CA 94111

tel 415-955-0663
fax 415-955-0676

4

KATIE NEILL
KATIE@800HIGHSTREET.COM
800 HIGH STREET
PALO ALTO, CA 94301
650.863.9800
800HIGHSTREET.COM

800
HIGH
STREET

1

design firm: Turnstyle
art director: Steve Watson
designer: Steve Watson
client: Serengeti
software/hardware: Adobe Illustrator
paper/materials: Fox River Starwhite Tiara Vellum 130 lb DTC

2

design firm: Ginger Griffin Marketing and Design
art director: Kara Hollinger
designer: Kara Hollinger
client: Sticki Rice
software/hardware: Adobe Illustrator CS2
paper/materials: Mohawk Navajo 100 lb, custom die-cut

3

design firm: Bakken Creative Co.
art director: Michelle Bakken
designer: Tae Hatayama
client: Perbacco Ristorante and Bar
software/hardware: Adobe Illustrator

4

design firm: Bakken Creative Co.
art director: Michelle Bakken
designer: Gina Mondello
client: Pacific Marketing Associates
software/hardware: Adobe Illustrator

1

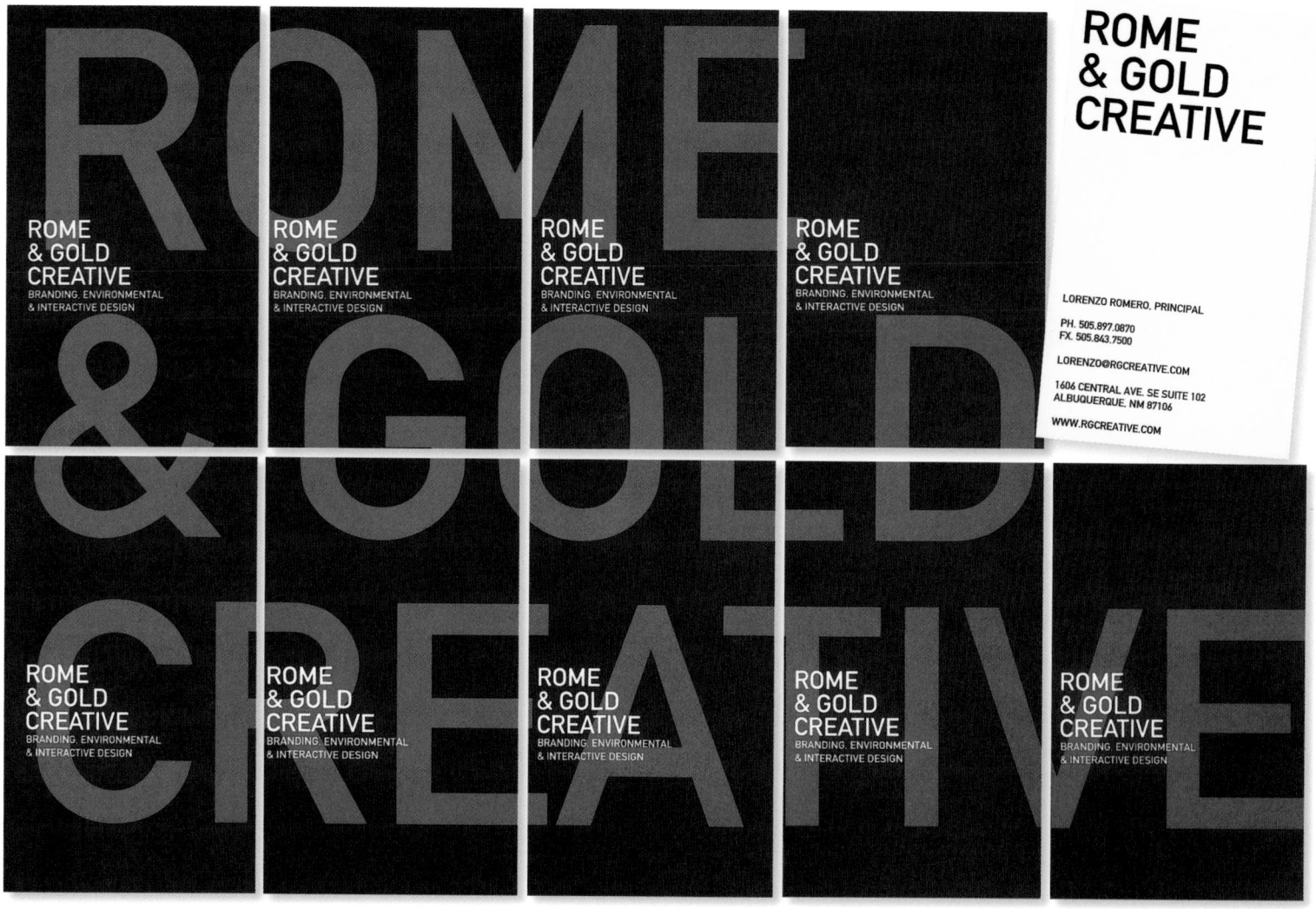
ROME & GOLD CREATIVE
BRANDING, ENVIRONMENTAL & INTERACTIVE DESIGN
ROME & GOLD CREATIVE
LORENZO ROMERO, PRINCIPAL
PH. 505.897.0870
FX. 505.843.7500
LORENZO@RGCREATIVE.COM
1606 CENTRAL AVE. SE SUITE 102
ALBUQUERQUE, NM 87106
WWW.RGCREATIVE.COM

2

3

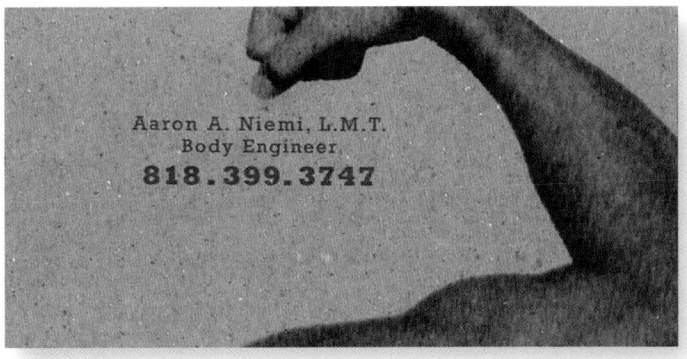

1

design firm: Rome & Gold Creative
art director: Robert Goldie
designer: Lorenzo Romero
client: Rome & Gold Creative
software/hardware: Adobe Illustrator
paper/materials: Neenah Classic Crest Natural, 130 lb cover

2

design firm: WOW Branding
art director: Perry Chua
designer: Will Johnson and Jeff Schramm
client: Invest Dubai
software/hardware: Adobe Illustrator
paper/materials: Classic Crest

3

design firm: Mingovits
client: Aaron Niemi, LMT
software/hardware: Adobe InDesign and Photoshop
paper/materials: Leftover packing board

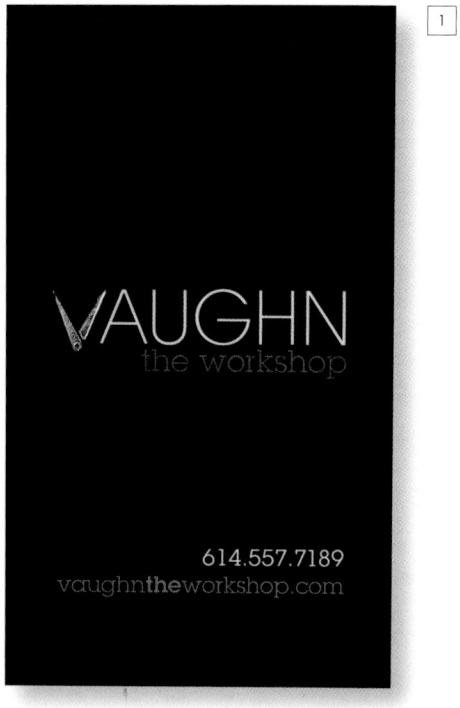
VAUGHN
the workshop
614.557.7189
vaughntheworkshop.com

1

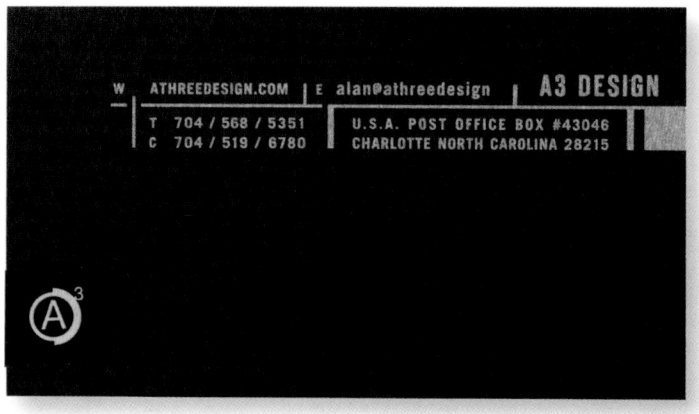
W ATHREEDESIGN.COM
E alan@athreedesign
A3 DESIGN
T 704 / 568 / 5351
C 704 / 519 / 6780
U.S.A. POST OFFICE BOX #43046
CHARLOTTE NORTH CAROLINA 28215

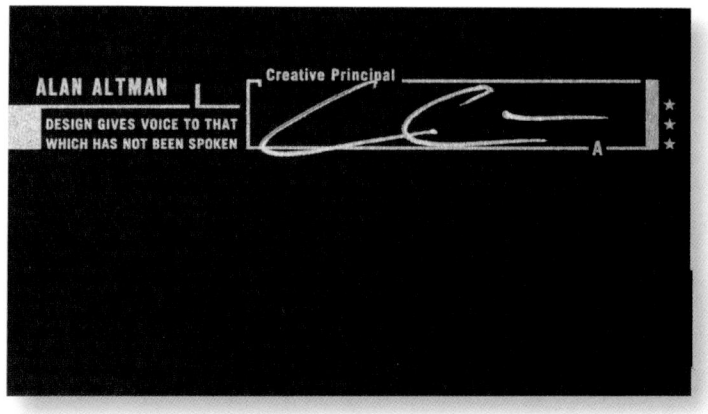
ALAN ALTMAN
Creative Principal
DESIGN GIVES VOICE TO THAT
WHICH HAS NOT BEEN SPOKEN

2

RUSSELL PINTADO PHOTOGRAPHY
504.485.0363 ruspinta@aol.com

3

4

1

design firm: Switch Creative
art director: Michael Carpenter
designer: Michael Carpenter
client: Vaughn the workshop
software/hardware: Adobe Illustrator
paper/materials: Silk cards and foil

2

design firm: A3 Design
art director: Amanda Altman
designer: Alan Altman
client: A3 Design
software/hardware: Adobe Illustrator

3

design firm: Louviere + Vanessa
art director: Jeff Louviere
designer: Jeff Louviere
client: Russell Pintado Photography
software/hardware: Adobe Illustrator and Photoshop
paper/materials: 2-color on Mohawk

4

design firm: Rome & Gold Creative
art director: Lorenzo Romero

Y
YOUN

KYEONG-WON YOUN
Art Director/Graphic Designer
7070 Grelot Rd #138
Mobile, AL 36695
251.776.7572(H)
251.461.1437(O)
kwyoun@hotmail.com
www.southalabama.edu/art/

1

www.georgefontenette.com

GEORGE
FONTENETTE
music composer_producer
mobile_551.998.6446
email_george@georgefontenette.com

2

3

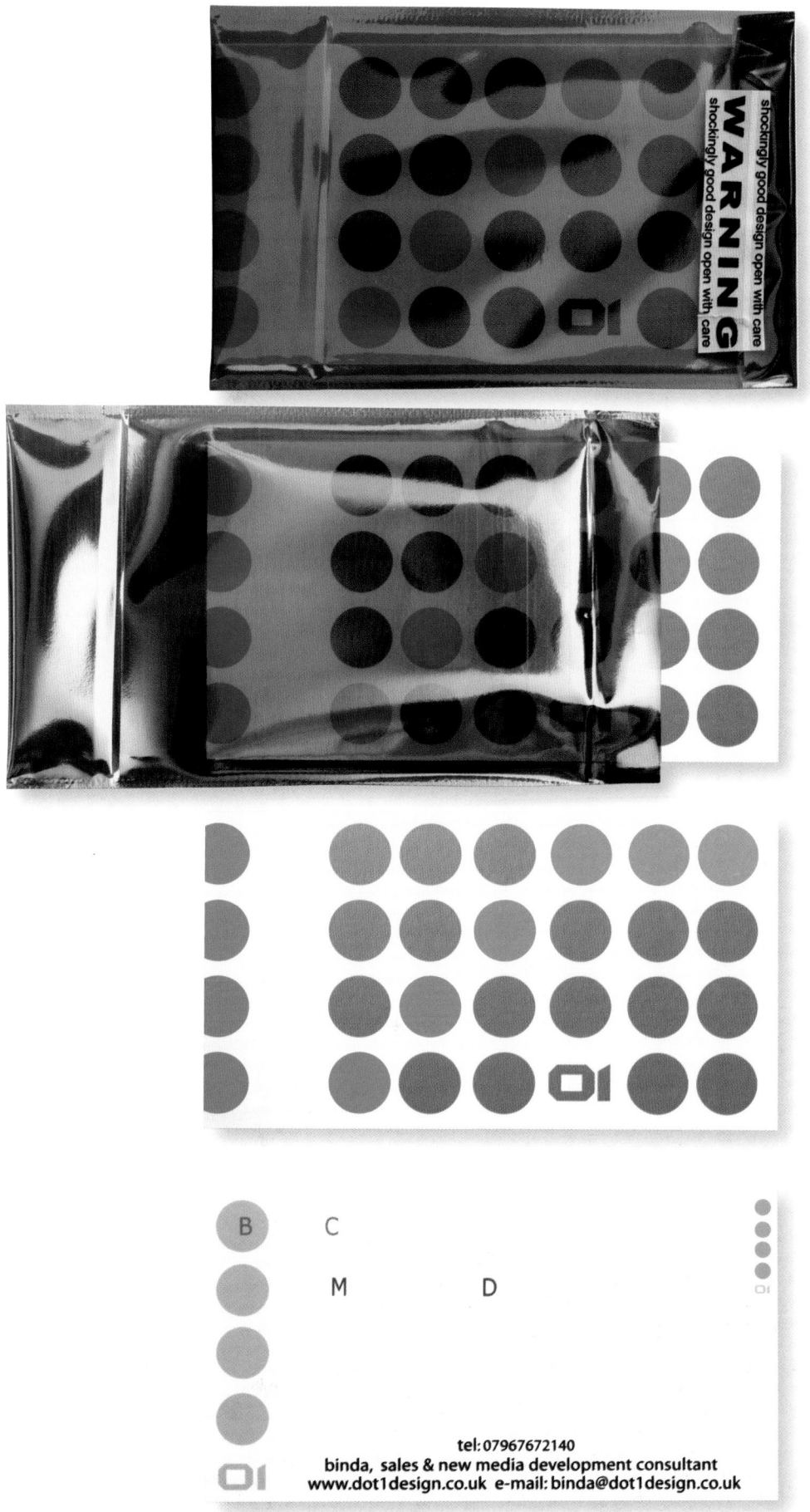
shockingly good design open with care
WARNING
shockingly good design open with care
B
C
M
D
tel: 07967672140
binda, sales & new media development consultant
www.dot1design.co.uk e-mail: binda@dot1design.co.uk

1

1

design firm: MBA
art director: Mark Brinkman and Mike Coffin
designer: Mark Brinkman and John Tullis
client: Havana
software/hardware: Adobe Creative Suite
paper/materials: Strathmore Natural White

2

design firm: Orangeseed Design
art director: Damien Wolf
designer: Rebecca Aviña
client: Orangeseed Design
software/hardware: Adobe Illustrator and Quark Xpress
paper/materials: Cougar White 100 lb cover

3

design firm: Fuel
designer: Bill Bollman, Lance Lethcoe, Patrick Prior, and Matt Kempel
client: Cedar Ridge Vineyards
software/hardware: Adobe Illustrator and Photoshop

2

Damien Wolf
dwolf@orangeseed.com
[PHN] 612-252-9757 x201
[FAX] 612-252-9760
800 Washington Ave. N., Suite 461
Minneapolis, MN 55401-1196
ORANGESEED

Damien Wolf
dwolf@orangeseed.com
[PHN] 612-252-9757 x201
[FAX] 612-252-9760
800 Washington Ave. N., Suite 461
Minneapolis, MN 55401-1196
ORANGESEED

Kristin Murra
kmurra@orangeseed.com
[PHN] 612-252-9757 x205
[FAX] 612-252-9760
800 Washington Ave. N., Suite 461
Minneapolis, MN 55401-1196
ORANGESEED

Kristin Murra
kmurra@orangeseed.com
[PHN] 612-252-9757 x205
[FAX] 612-252-9760
800 Washington Ave. N., Suite 461
Minneapolis, MN 55401-1196
ORANGESEED

3

CEDAR
RIDGE
VINEYARDS

CEDAR RIDGE VINEYARDS, LLC
WINERY & DISTILLERY
VINEYARD MANAGER
ELLIOT WILSON
elliot@crwine.com
LOCATION
501 7th Avenue SE
Suite B
CEDAR RAPIDS
IA
52401
319-362-2778 FAX 319-362-2827
CRWINE.COM

nine lives
reincarnated furniture & accessories

nine lives
reincarnated furniture & accessories

1

nine lives

nine lives
reincarnated furniture & accessories
103 main street
parkville, missouri 64152
816·741·4448

2

DRY™ www.drysoda.com

SODA CO: SHARELLE KLAUS / FOUNDER & CEO
T/F 253.573.0197 / M 253.970.8201 / E sharelle@drysoda.com
715 North J Street / Tacoma, WA 98403

3

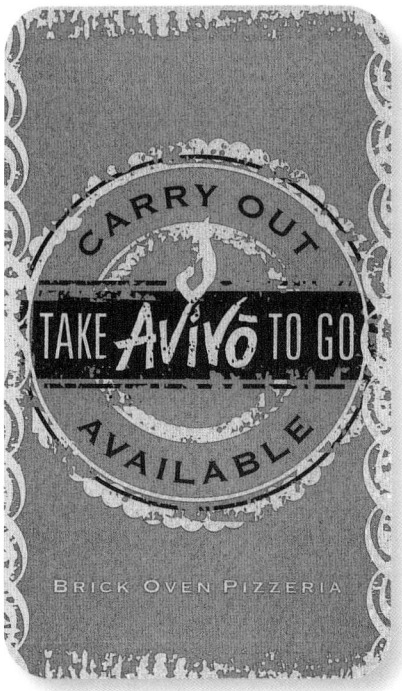

4

WWW.JASMINEBLACK.COM JASMINEBLACKPAPER@YAHOO.COM

Jasmine black
PAPER + GIFT

JENNIFER BLACK	3703 KERBEY LANE, AUSTIN 78731 512 420-2680 TO FAX JUST ADD 1	JASON SCHUBERT

1

design firm: Design Ranch
art director: Michelle Sonderegger & Ingrid Sidie
designer: Michelle Sonderegger
client: Nine Lives
software/hardware: Adobe Illustrator

2

design firm: Turnstyle
art director: Steve Watson
designer: Steve Watson
client: Dry Soda
software/hardware: Adobe Illustrator
paper/materials: Fox River Starwhite Tiara Vellum 130 lb DTC

3

design firm: Entermotion Design Studio
designer: Lea Morrow
client: Avivo Brick Oven Pizza and In the Sauce Brands
software/hardware: Macromedia Freehand
paper/materials: Domtar Feltweave, 3 color

4

design firm: Shoehorn
designer: Will Hornaday
client: Jasmine Black Paper and Gift
software/hardware: Adobe Illustrator CS
paper/materials: Classic Crest Windsor Blue 80 lb cover

VIVENDI
DEVELOPMENT
WWW.VIVENDIDEVELOPMENT.COM

KEITH B. PERRY
MANAGING DIRECTOR
TEL 919 785 0777
FAX 919 785 0775
4804 SWEETBRIAR DR, RALEIGH, NC 27609
PO BOX 20250, RALEIGH, NC 27619
KPERRY@VIVENDIDEVELOPMENT.COM

1

LIFE * ART
iungo
210 215 8789
ROLANDO G. MURILLO
x
www.goiungo.com

GET INTO
THE RIGHT
FRAME OF
MIND
WWW.GOIUNGO.COM

2

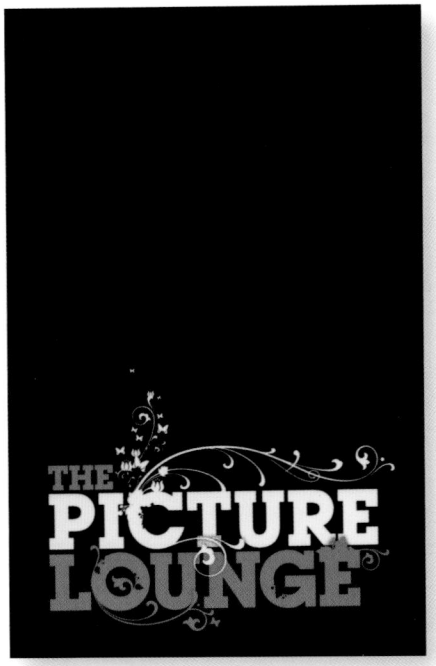

3

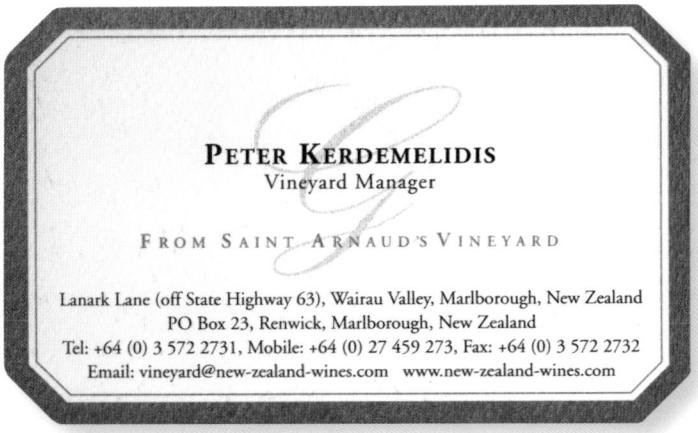

4

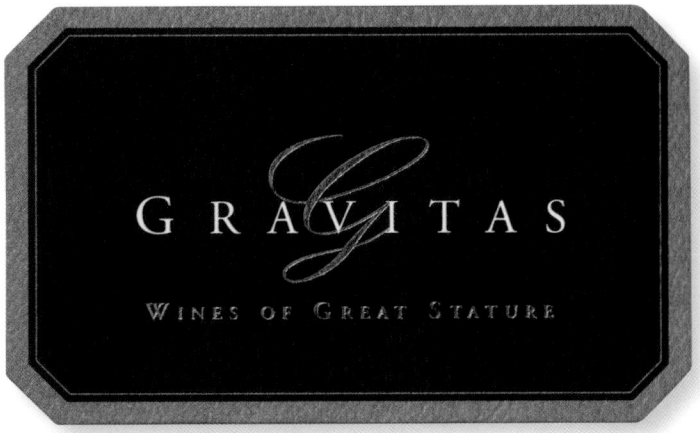

1

design firm: Helena Seo Design
art director: Helena Seo
designer: Helena Seo
client: Vivendi Development
software/hardware: Adobe Illustrator
paper/materials: Starwhite Sirius Smooth 130 lb DTC

2

design firm: Murillo Design, Inc.
art director: Roland Murillo
designer: Roland Murillo
client: Iungo Arts Magazine
paper/materials: Mohawk Superfine Eggshell White 120 DTC

3

design firm: Creative Spark
art director: Art director: Andy Mallalieu
designer: Andy Mallalieu
client: The Picture Lounge/ Jamilla Paul
software/hardware: Adobe Illustrator
paper/materials: 300 gsm, silk paper, high gloss finish, metallic gold ink

4

design firm: Lloyds Graphic Design Ltd.
art director: Alexander Lloyd
designer: Alexander Lloyd
client: Gravitas
software/hardware: Macromedia Freehand
paper/materials: Sundance Ultrawhite 270 gsm

1

limb design

success by design Limb Design

Elise De Silva
Principal

7026 Old Katy Road - Suite 350
Houston, Texas 77024

tel 713 529 1117 cell 713 703 7624

elise@limbdesign.com
www.limbdesign.com

2

Elizabeth Arrington
www.arringtonphotography.net
info@arringtonphotography.net
512.468.5661

Photo Journalism · Advertising · Weddings · Graduations · Portraits
On Location · Studio · B&W · Color

3

Julie Challman
Software Engineer

Parametric™
Leaders in Structured Portfolio Management

1151 Fairview Avenue North
Seattle, WA 98109-4418

T 206 694 5516
F 206 694 5566
E jchallman@paraport.com

www.parametricportfolio.com

4

KEVIN AKERS
13 HART STREET
SAN RAFAEL, CA
ZIP 94901-2605
HOME 415.459.3424
STUDIO 415.455.0562
FAX 415.455.0597
MODEM 415.459.4767

1

design firm: Limb Design
art director: Emilie Gruson
designer: Emilie Gruson
client: Limb Design
software/hardware: Adobe InDesign
paper/materials: Mohawk Superfine

2

design firm: Lolight Design
art director: Aaron Deckler
designer: Aaron Deckler
client: Arrington Photography
software/hardware: Adobe Photoshop and InDesign

3

design firm: Turnstyle
art director: Ben Graham
designer: Jason Gomez
client: Parametric
software/hardware: Adobe Illustrator
paper/materials: Mohawk Strathmore Ultimate White 110 lb cover

4

design firm: Kevin Akers Design and Imagery
art director: Kevin Akers
designer: Kevin Akers
illustrator: Kevin Akers
client: Kevin Akers
software/hardware: Adobe Illustrator

THE HENLEY COLLEGE LIBRARY

1

tanja_devetak
gornji trg 1_ljubljana
+386.1.426.95.90
pon-pet 10-13 in 16-19_sob 10-13

tanja_devetak
gornji trg 1_ljubljana
+386.1.426.95.90
pon-pet 10-13 in 16-19_sob 10-13

tanja_devetak
gornji trg 1_ljubljana
+386.1.426.95.90
pon-pet 10-13 in 16-19_sob 10-13

tanja_devetak
gornji trg 1_ljubljana
+386.1.426.95.90
pon-pet 10-13 in 16-19_sob 10-13

Clark W. Morris EXECUTIVE DIRECTOR
morrisc@harriman-jewell.org
www.harriman-jewell.org
p 816·415·5997
f 816·415·5035

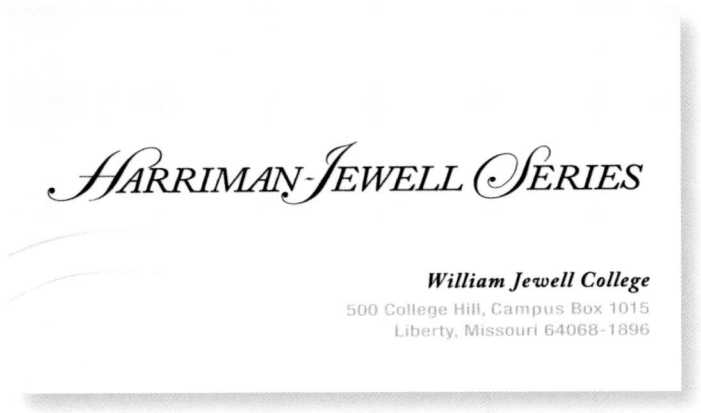
2
HARRIMAN-JEWELL SERIES
William Jewell College
500 College Hill, Campus Box 1015
Liberty, Missouri 64068-1896

3
BLACK HORSE
Capital
Dale B.
MANAGING
45 ROCKEFELLER P
NEW YORK, NEW
telephone 212 332.1112 facsimile 212 332.1113
email DCHAPPELL@BLACKHORSECAP.COM

1

FIONA GUY ACIPR

E • fiona@impactmediapr.com
M • 07974 722275

MM2 Building • 84 Pickford Street
Manchester • M4 5BT

T • +44 (0) 161 236 0008
F • +44 (0) 161 236 0204
W • www.impactmediapr.com

impact mediapr

CIPR MEMBER

2

home
Ben Hickman Creative Director
a: 71 fleetwood avenue westcliff on sea essex ss0 9rb
phone home: +44 (0)1702 344692 m: +44 (0)7703 444764
e: info@homecreatives.com w: www.homecreatives.com

3

Links SM
FITNESS
a signature fitness center
104 ARMOUR ROAD, NORTH KANSAS CITY, MO 64116
816-842-3200 : 816-221-1829 FAX : www.linksfitness.com

dvaughan@linksfitness.com
DOUG VAUGHAN
CHIEF EXECUTIVE OFFICER
913-638-3542 MOBILE

1

Donna Ferrentino
T: 718-852-3017
C: 917-519-9204
www.soulpicnicinteractive.com
E: donna@soulpicnicinteractive.com
IM dferrentino
soulpicnic interactive

2

CHRIS KNEIFEL
D 702.727.4607 x306
C 480.231.0427
E CSK@VEGASGRANDPRIX.COM
201 S. LAS VEGAS BLVD., STE. 150
LAS VEGAS, NEVADA 89101
RACE TRACK MANAGER >>
VEGAS
GRAND PRIX

GRANDPRIX
ARIZONA
TOM TYGETT >>
D 602.889.3091 x308
C 602.526.5888
E TOMT@GRANDPRIXARIZONA.COM
6245 N. 24TH PKWY. STE 207, PHOENIX, AZ 85016
OPERATIONS

3

1

design firm: Think Studio, NYC
art director: John Clifford
designer: John Clifford
client: Soulpicnic Interactive
software/hardware: Adobe Illustrator and Quark Xpress
paper/materials: Mohawk Superfine

2

design firm: Campbell Fisher Design
art director: Greg Fisher
designer: Stacy Crawford and Ashley Flanagan
client: Champ Car
software/hardware: Adobe Illustrator
paper/materials: Classic Crest 165 lb cover

3

design firm: Base Art Co.
art director: Terry Rohrbach
designer: Terry Rohrbach
client: Base Art Co.
software/hardware: Adobe InDesign
paper/materials: Acrylic

1

AUBURN RIDGE

Finely Crafted Kitchens, Cabinets, and Millwork

BOB RENFORTH
CABINET AND MILLWORK SPECIALIST

2424 RIMROCK ROAD
MADISON, WI 53713
BRENFORTH@AUBURNRIDGE.COM

TEL 866/473/4925
CELL 608/209/4163
FAX 608/655/3553

WWW.AUBURNRIDGE.COM

2

Morrow & Co.LLC
CERTIFIED PUBLIC ACCOUNTANTS

Richard L. Morrow CPA
PHONE 316.263.2223 FAX 316.263.2302
421 EAST 3RD STREET NORTH ▪ WICHITA, KS 67202
E rich@morrowandcompany.com

ACCOUNTING FOR YOUR NEEDS℠
www.morrowandcompany.com

3

TM

TRADEMARK™
PACKAGING
A Division of First Pacific Enterprises Inc.

E steve@trademarkpackaging.com TF 1 888 545 3090
T 250 545 3098 F 250 545 3239 C 250 212 9094
W www.trademarkpackaging.com

STEVE HARVEY
NATIONAL SALES MGR.

Our Packaging is your Trademark™

USA | CANADA

CANADA Suite 600, 280 Nelson St, Vancouver, BC V6B 2E2
USA 305 North Harbor Blvd, San Pedro, CA 90731

4

THE
DESIGN FIRM

Luke Despatie

One Vancouver Avenue, Toronto, ON M4L 2S7
416.995.0243 luke@thedesignfirm.ca

www.thedesignfirm.ca

1

design firm: Shine Advertising
art director: Mike Kriefski, John Krull
designer: Emilie Smith
client: Auburn Ridge

2

design firm: Entermotion Design Studio
designer: Lea Morrow
client: Morrow and Company
software/hardware: Macromedia Freehand

3

design firm: Dossier Creative, Inc.
art director: Don Chisholm
designer: Patrick Smith
client: Trademark Packaging
software/hardware: Adobe Illustrator and InDesign
paper/materials: Mohawk Navajo Brilliant White 120 lb cover

4

design firm: The Design Firm
art director: Luke Despatie
designer: Luke Despatie
client: The Design Firm
software/hardware: Quark Xpress
paper/materials: Neenah Classic Crest

1

1

design firm: Design Ranch
art director: Michelle Sonderegger and Igred Sidie
designer: Ted Carpenter and Rachel Karaca
client: Bennett Schneider

bennett schneider
specialty greetings & paper
merikay lott
loc 311 east 55th street _ kansas city, missouri 64113
tele 816.444.8484 _ mail ml@bennettschneider.com
fax 816.444.3115 _ web bennettschneider.com

bennett schneider
specialty greetings & paper
loc 311 east 55th street _ kansas city, missouri 64113
tele 816.444.8484 _ mail info@bennettschneider.com
fax 816.444.3115 _ web bennettschneider.com

bennett schneider
specialty greetings & paper

1

2

1

design firm: Miles Design
art director: Josh Miles
designer: Eric Folzenlogel
client: Surroundings

2

design firm: Ginger Griffin Marketing and Design
art director: Kara Hollinger
designer: Eddy Herty and Kara Hollinger

3

design firm: Sheriff Design
art director: Paul Sheriff
designer: Paul Sheriff
client: Patti Dougherty

3

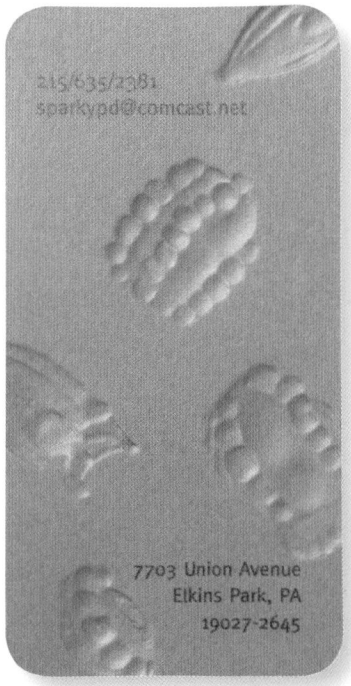
215/635/2381
sparkypd@comcast.net
7703 Union Avenue
Elkins Park, PA
19027-2645

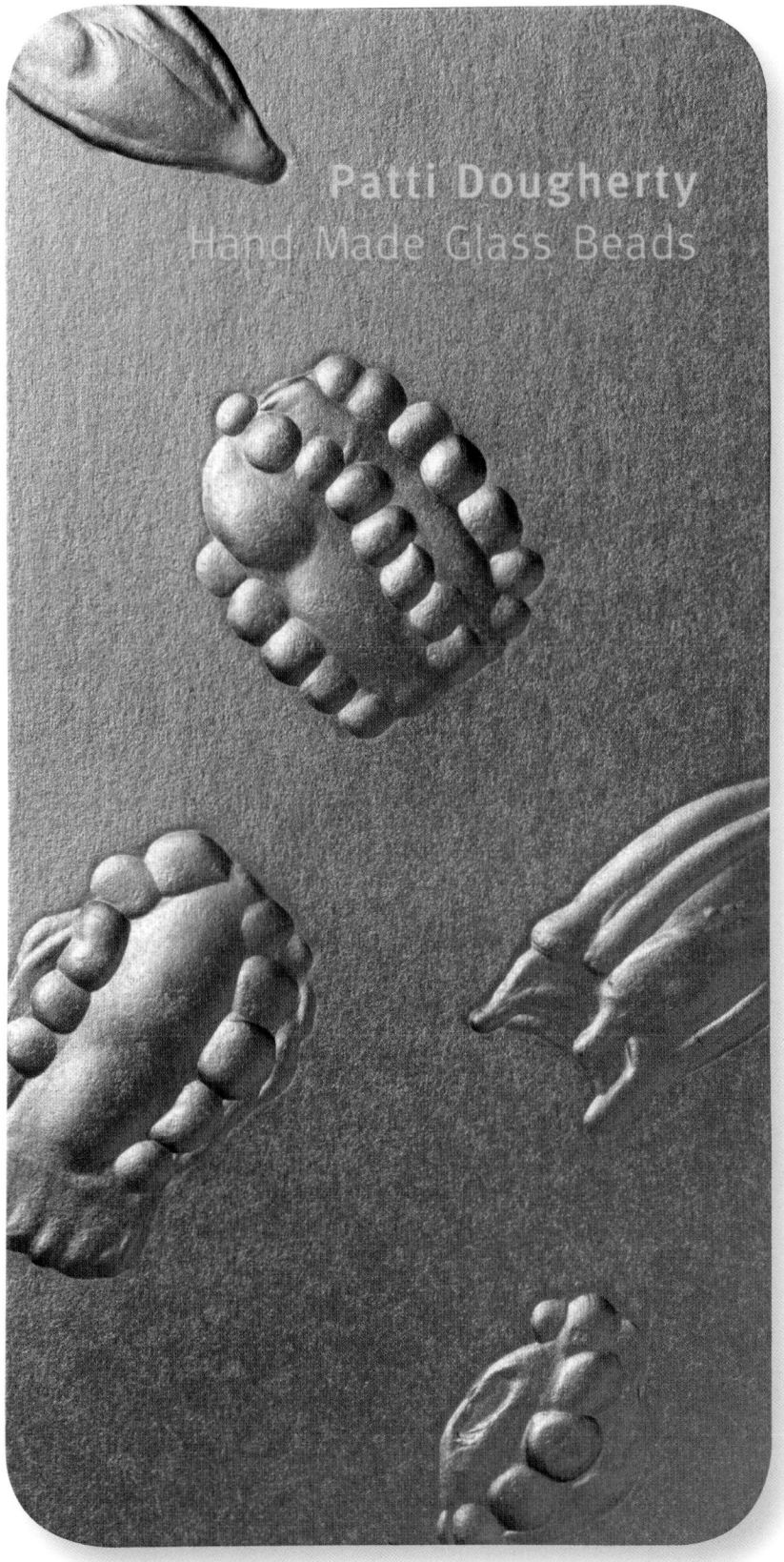
Patti Dougherty
Hand Made Glass Beads

Clothes & accessories for the discerning glamourpuss
7 Old Bank Street Manchester M2 7PE / 0161 832 8595
5 Exchange Street St Ann's Square Manchester M2 7EE / 0161 819 1614
165 Halle Mall The Arndale Centre Manchester M4 3AB / 0161 834 5806
73 Church Street Liverpool L1 1DG / 0151 707 9574
pastiche

1

it's easy
being green

frogfile
Gil Yaron
gil@frogfile.com
Frogfile Office Essentials
480 Melmore Road, P.O. Box 335
Bowen Island, BC V0N 1G0
t: 604 947 6929
f: 604 947 6949
www.frogfile.com

2

3

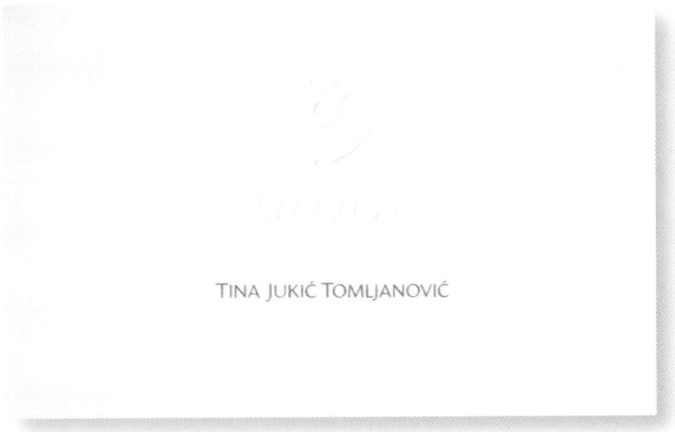

4

1

design firm: Imagine
art director: David Caunce
designer: David Caunce
client: Pastiche
software/hardware: Adobe Illustrator
paper/materials: 300 gsm, matte, lamination

2

design firm: smashLAB
art director: Eric Karjaluoto
designer: Peter Pimentel
illustrator: Peter Pimentel
client: Frogfile Office Essentials
software/hardware: Adobe Illustrator
paper/materials: Vegetable-based inks,
processed chlorine-free
100% post-consumer waste
Save-A-Tree paper

3

design firm: Elevator
art director: Tony Adamic
designer: Tony Adamic and Lana Vitas
client: Ulola
software/hardware: Adobe Illustrator
paper/materials: Conqueror Stonemarquee

4

design firm: Detail Design Studio
art director: Detail Design Studio
designer: Detail Design Studio
client: The Ark:
A Cultural Centre for Children
software/hardware: Adobe Illustrator
and Quark Xpress
paper/materials: Splendorgel

1

THE
katalyst
CONSULTANCY
kevin carroll, katalyst
503.807.2401
pmb 341 • 9220 sw barbur blvd • #119
portland, oregon • 97219
kc@katalystconsultancy.com

68
Dr+
Dreamer
199.1109
8
06
4
04
14
1

2

SPI
HOME
377 SWIFT AVENUE, SOUTH SAN FRANCISCO, CA 94080
WWW.SPI-HOME.COM
ERIC CHEN
vice president / general manager
tel 650 616 7777 / 800 223 4438 x 225
fax 650 616 4800 / 800 223 4428
email ERICCHEN@SPI-HOME.COM

1

design firm: Willoughby Design Group
art director: Deb Tagtalianidis and Ann Willoughby (Creative director)
designer: Lindsay Laricks
client: Kevin Carroll

2

design firm: Helena Seo Design
art director: Helena Seo
designer: Helena Seo
client: SPI Home
software/hardware: Adobe Illustrator
paper/materials: Crane's 134 lb cover, Pearl White Kid Finish

3

design firm: Miriello Grafico
art director: Dennis Garcia
designer: Sallie Reynolds Allen
client: Yoga Fuzion
software/hardware: Adobe Illustrator
paper/materials: French Smart White 110 lb cover

CANAL
ASSOCIATES LLC
Distinctive City Residences
Mike McCurley
Partner
T 301.343.7331
F 301.215.6453
E mmccurley@canalassociates.com
7110 Exfair Rd.
Bethesda, MD 20814
www.canalassociates.com

1

ROGER ALLEN
Roger Allen Design + Photo
Website: www.rager1.com
E.mail: rager1@mac.com
Vancouver, B.C. Canada
604.738.7696

2

3

4

1

design firm: Jill Tanenbaum Graphic Design & Advertising Inc.
designer: Jennifer Prophet
client: Canal Associates LLC
software/hardware: Adobe Illustrator, InDesign, and Photoshop
paper/materials: Strathmore Natural White 80 lb cover

2

design firm: Rager 1
art director: Roger Allen
designer: Roger Allen
client: Roger Allen
software/hardware: Adobe InDesign
paper/materials: Silk Screen

3

design firm: KBDA
art director: Kim Baer
designer: Keith Knueven
client: Buddha Jones
software/hardware: Adobe Creative Suite

4

design firm: Willoughby Design Group
art director: Deb Tagtalianidis and Ann Willoughby (Creative director)
designer: Zack Shubkagel and Hammerpress
client: SPIN! Neapolitan Pizza

1

Journée
ICONDUCTOR ILLUMINATION
NATE QUAN
VP-SALES & OPERATIONS
n.quan@jrne.com
WWW.JOURNEELIGHTING.COM
TELEPHONE 800-886-1880 - FAX 800-886-1881
4607 Lakeview Canyon Rd #500 - Westlake Village, CA 91361

2

PRICE FIGHT
www.pricefight.com
F: MICHAEL
L: GRIFFIN
michael@pricefight.com
401 E. 53RD ST. #103
AUSTIN, TX 78751
(800) 929-4062
Shop like a Champ.
PRICE FIGHT

3

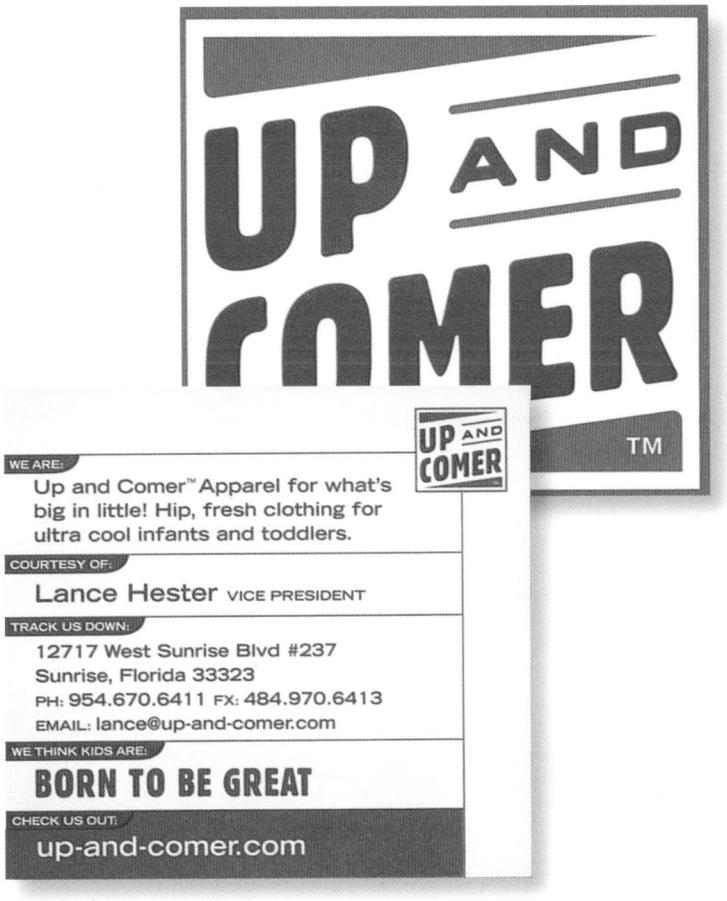

4

1

design firm: Reactor
art director: Clifton Alexander
designer: Clifton Alexander
client: Journée Lighting
software/hardware: Adobe Illustrator
paper/materials: Endeavor Velvet, embossed

2

design firm: Adlucent
art director: Nicholas Herman
designer: Nicholas Herman
illustrator: Nicholas Herman
client: PriceFight.com
software/hardware: Adobe Illustrator, Mac
paper/materials: 3 color and die-cut on Cougar Opaque, polyester laser labels

3

design firm: Alphabet Arm Design
designer: Aaron Belyea
client: Up and Comer™
software/hardware: Adobe Illustrator

4

design firm: Julia Reich Design
art director: Julia Reich
designer: Julia Reich
client: Julia Reich Design
software/hardware: Quark Xpress
printing: Terrance Chouinard, Wells College Book Arts Center

Dustin Hassard
8803542673
8199808710
Dustin@BandFly.com
bandfly
Design +
Marketing
& Music

1

El
CHILE
Cafe y Cantina
Carlos Rivero
Operator
512/457-9900
1809 Manor Rd.
Austin, Texas 78722

2

MINDFUL REVOLUTION
LEIGH-ANNE BROWN
certified yoga instructor & MEd
PHONE: 512-416-8008
LA@mindfulrevolution.com
MINDFULREVOLUTION.COM

3

4

1

design firm: Brandfly
art director: Dustin Hassard
designer: Dustin Hassard
client: Bandfly
software/hardware: Adobe Illustrator
paper/materials: Plastic

2

design firm: Zócalo Design
art director: Blake Trabulsi
client: El Chile Cafe y Cantina
software/hardware: Adobe InDesign

3

design firm: The Decoder Ring Design Concern
art director: Paul Fucik
designer: Paul Fucik
client: Mindful Revolution
software/hardware: Adobe Illustrator
paper/materials: 2/2 color on Cougar Natural 80 lb cover

4

design firm: Judson Design
art director: Jeff Davis
designer: Jeff Davis
client: Davis Guide Service
software/hardware: Adobe CS2
paper/materials: Astrolite, PMS red and black

1

substance

substance

IDA CHEINMAN_PRINCIPAL_CREATIVE DIRECTOR_
2304 E. Baltimore St. P 410 732 8379 ida@substance151.com
Baltimore MD 21224 F 425 940 7800 www.substance151.com
INTEGRATED VISUAL COMMUNICATIONS

IDA CHEINMAN_PRINCIPAL_CREATIVE DIRECTOR_
2304 E. Baltimore St. P 410 732 8379 ida@substance151.com
Baltimore MD 21224 F 425 940 7800 www.substance151.com
INTEGRATED VISUAL COMMUNICATIONS

2

High Performance Data Integration
eti
eti
Ron Baker
President & CEO
512.383.3100 mobile: 310.433.2400
816 Congress, 14th Floor Austin, Texas 78701
main: 512.383.3000 fax: 512.383.3306
rbaker@eti.com www.eti.com

3

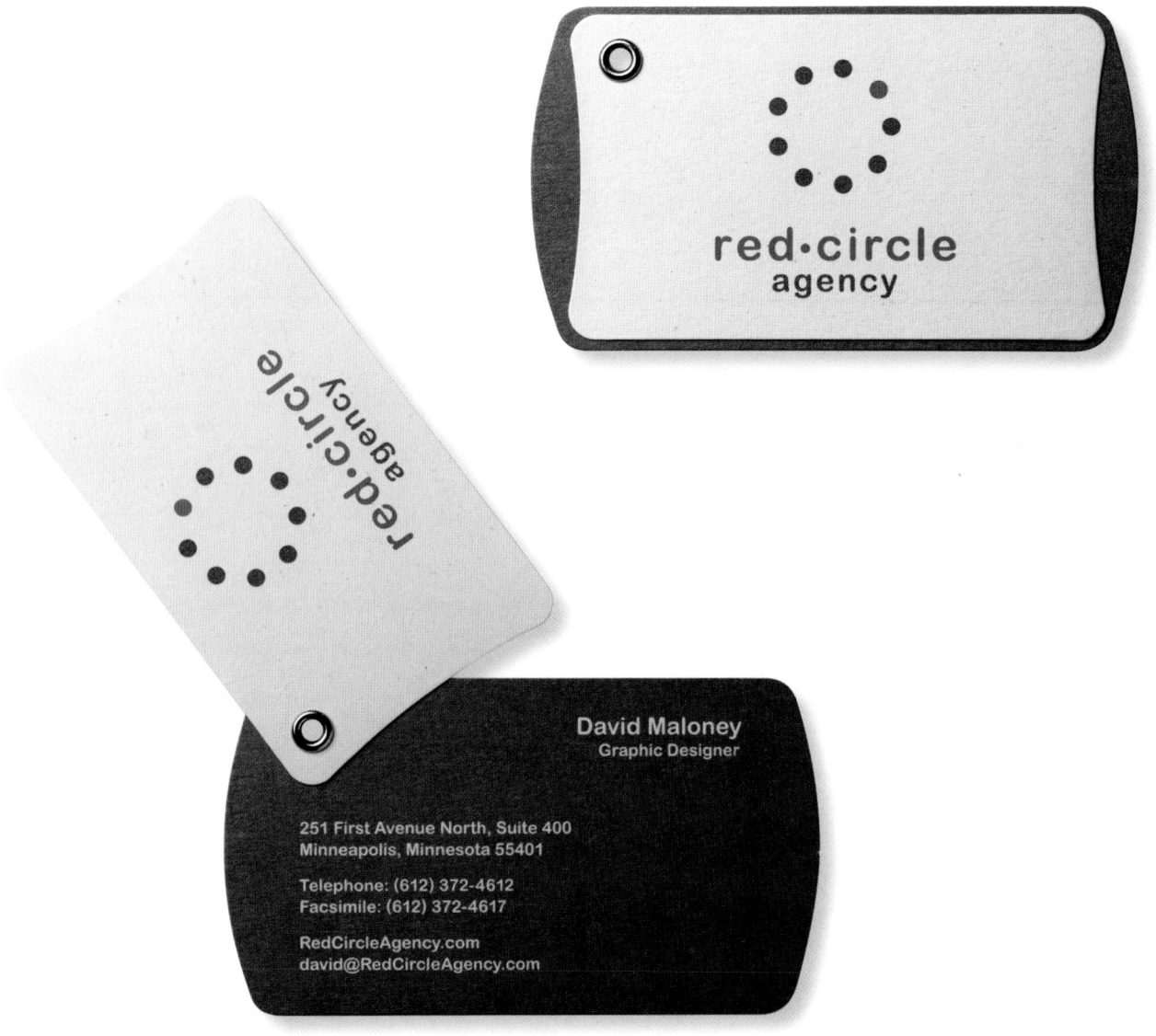

1

design firm: substance151
art director: Ida Cheinman
designer: Ida Cheinman and Rick Salzman
client: substance151
software/hardware: Adobe Illustrator
paper/materials: Mohawk Navajo, 3/3 colors, metallic ink

2

design firm: MBA
art director: Mark Brinkman and Mike Coffin
designer: Mark Brinkman and Caroline Pledger
client: ETI
software/hardware: Adobe Creative Suite
paper/materials: Monadnock Astrolite smooth

3

design firm: Red Circle Agency
art director: David Maloney
designer: David Maloney
client: Red Circle Agency
software/hardware: Adobe Illustrator and InDesign
paper/materials: Hand-set eyelet

1
GLENN WILSON
GLENN@FLAVORLEAGUE.COM
TASTY HANDSCREENED WALLCOVERINGS
EST.1970
[SORT OF...]
FLAVOR PAPER
4213 CHARTRES ST.
NEW ORLEANS LA 70117
504
944.0447 TEL
944.0484 FAX
261.6660 CEL
ER.COM
EMILY R. MITCHELL
EMILY@FLAVORLEAGUE.COM
TASTY HANDSCREENED WALLCOVERINGS
EST.1970
[SORT OF...]
FLAVOR PAPER
4213 CHARTRES ST.
NEW ORLEANS LA 70117
504
944.0447 TEL
944.0484 FAX
621.7980 CEL
ER.COM
JOSEPH PERAINO, JR.
JOE@FLAVORLEAGUE.COM
TASTY HANDSCREENED WALLCOVERINGS
EST.1970
[SORT OF...]
FLAVOR PAPER
4213 CHARTRES ST.
NEW ORLEANS LA 70117
504
944.0447 TEL
944.0484 FAX
813.1823 CEL
ER.COM
JON SHERMAN
JON@FLAVORLEAGUE.COM
TASTY HANDSCREENED WALLCOVERINGS
EST.1970
[SORT OF...]
FLAVOR PAPER
4213 CHARTRES ST.
NEW ORLEANS LA 70117
504
944.0447 TEL
944.0484 FAX
975.7327 CEL
ER.COM

1

design firm: Zande + Newman Design
art director: Adam Newman
designer: Adam Newman and Loren Stephens
client: Flavor League
software/hardware: Adobe Illustrator and Photoshop
paper/materials: Mohawk Superfine

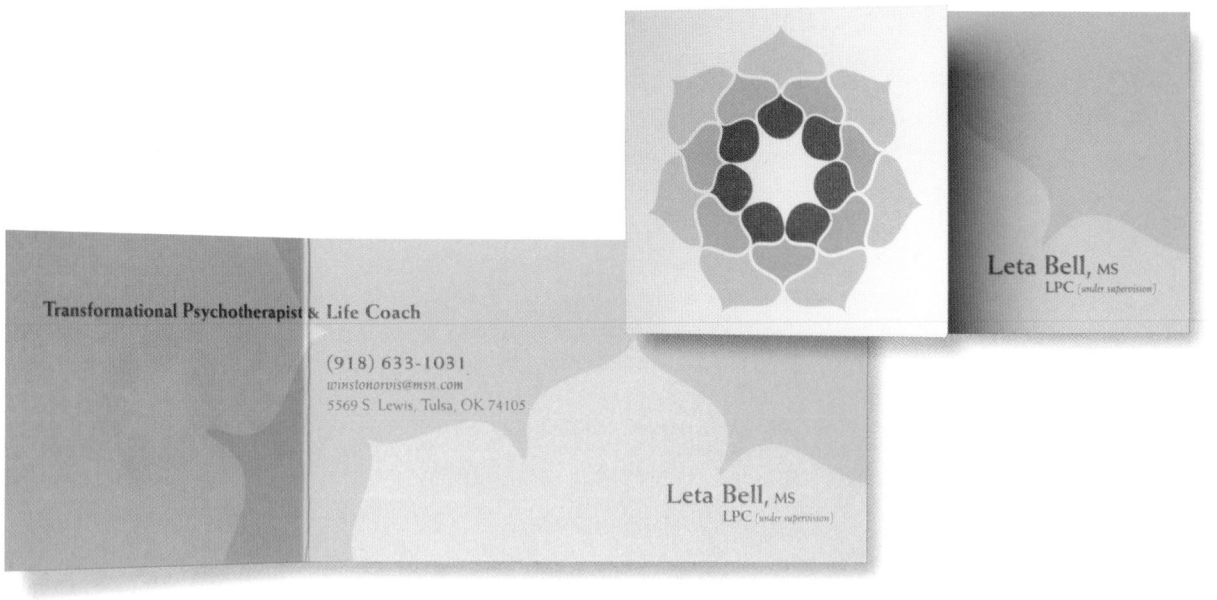
Transformational Psychotherapist & Life Coach
(918) 633-1031
winstonrvis@msn.com
5569 S. Lewis, Tulsa, OK 74105
Leta Bell, MS
LPC (under supervision)
Leta Bell, MS
LPC (under supervision)

1

vuru™
supplements made easy

Grant M Kornman
chief executive officer
gkornman@vuru.com
203 nw 36th street
miami, florida 33127
tel 305.576.0236 x 300
tel 1.877.get.vuru
cell 786.897.6766
fax 305.576.0282
www.vuru.com

2

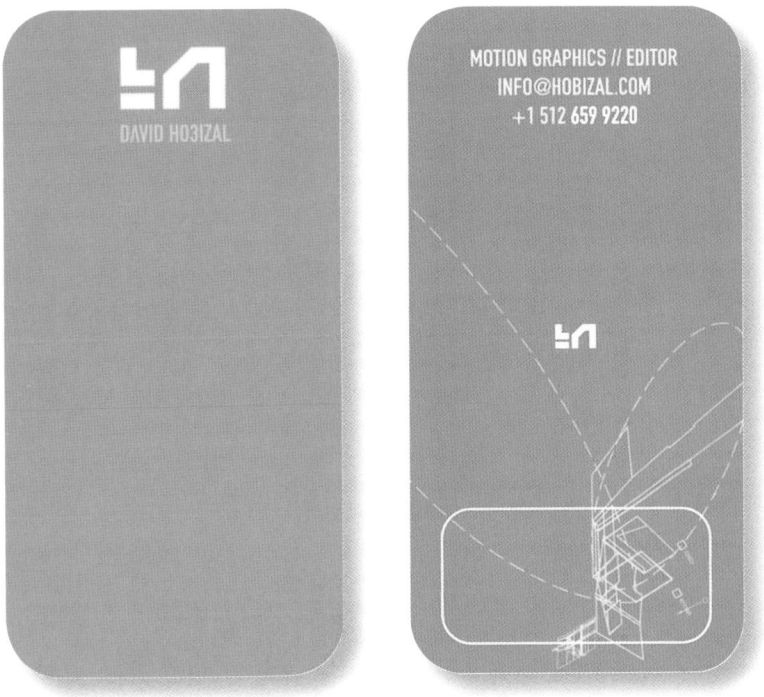

3

1

design firm: David Clark Design
art director: David Clark
designer: Becky Gelder
client: Leta Bell
software/hardware: Adobe Illustrator CS
paper/materials: Classic Crest Solar White 80 lb cover
printing: McNally Printing, Tulsa, OK

2

design firm: Crave, Inc.
art director: David Edmundson
designer: Russ Martin
client: Vuru

4

3

design firm: Foda Studio
art director: Jett Butler
designer: Jett Butler
client: David Hobizal, Motion Graphics Editor
software/hardware: Adobe Illustrator
paper/materials: 2/1 C2S Satin Laminate

4

design firm: Turnstyle
art director: Ben Graham
designer: Ben Graham
client: Venue
software/hardware: Adobe Illustrator
paper/materials: Mohawk Options True White 100 lb cover

1

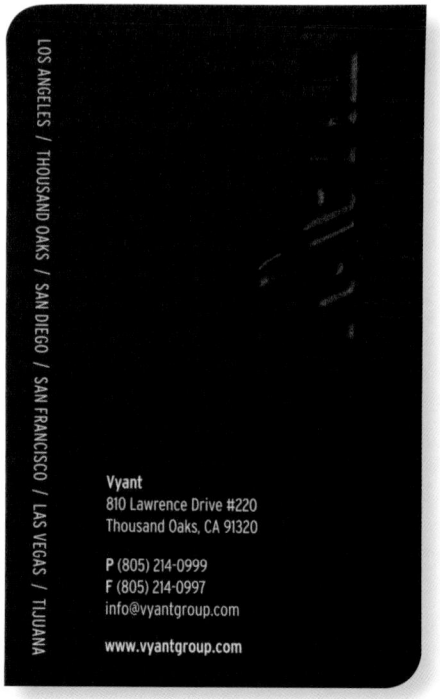

2

1

design firm: BR
art director: Franklin Oviedo, Anthony Magliano
designer: Franklin Oviedo, Anthony Magliano
client: Charlotte Street Foundation
software/hardware: Adobe Illustrator
paper/materials: Classic Crest Natural

2

design firm: Vyant Group
art director: Dave Carlson
designer: Catherine Reisen
client: Vyant Group
software/hardware: Adobe Illustrator
paper/materials: Mohawk

3

design firm: Dean Johnson Design
art director: Scott Johnson
designer: Ryan Abegglen
client: Dean Johnson Design
software/hardware: Adobe Illustrator and Photoshop
paper/materials: Cougar Smooth 120 lb cover

DEAN JOHNSON
DEAN JOHNSON

3

DEAN JOHNSON
646 MASSACHUSETTS AVENUE
INDIANAPOLIS, INDIANA 46204
T: 317.634.8020
F: 317.634.8054
DEANJOHNSON.COM
SCOTT JOHNSON
SJOHNSON@DEANJOHNSON.COM
DEAN JOHNSON

1

MARILYN STRAUSS
FOUNDER
TEL 816 531.7728
FAX 531.1911
4800 MAIN ST. STE.302
KANSAS CITY, MO 64112
WWW.KCSHAKES.ORG
HEART OF AMERICA
SHAKESPEARE FESTIVAL

2

the
DECODER
RING
ASK@THEDECODERRING.COM
P: 512-933-0079 F: 512-597-1848
WWW.THEDECODERRING.COM

3

4

1

design firm: BR
art director: Nathaniel Cooper
designer: Nathaniel Cooper
client: Heart of America Shakespeare Festival
software/hardware: Adobe Illustrator, InDesign, and Photoshop
paper/materials: Spray paint, chipboard

2

design firm: The Decoder Ring Design Concern
designer: Christian Helms
client: The Decoder Ring
software/hardware: Adobe Illustrator and Photoshop
paper/materials: Cougar Opaque

3

design firm: Design Ranch
art director: Michelle Sonderegger and Ingred Sidie
designer: Tad Carpenter
client: Raeta Estates
software/hardware: Adobe Illustrator

4

design firm: Di Depux
art director: Despina Bournele
designer: Despina Bournele
client: Erato
software/hardware: Adobe Illustrator CS
paper/materials: 1 Pantone, 1 metal Majestic F098, 250 gsm

THE HENLEY COLLEGE LIBRARY

1

MIXOLOGY 101

the
TOM COLLINS

Fill a Collins glass with ice.
You can build this one right
in the glass.

1 oz. Gin
Fill glass with equal amounts:
Sweet & Sour
Soda Water

Garnish with a cherry and
a lime squeeze.

MIXOLOGY 101

the
COSMOPOLITAN

1 1/2 oz. Vodka
1/2 oz. Cointreau or Triple Sec
3/4 oz. Lime Juice

Combine all the ingredients
in a cocktail shaker filled with
ice. Shake well. Strain into a
cocktail glass and garnish with
a lime squeeze.

HILLERY PEREZ
Mixologist

TABC CERTIFIED BARTENDING
FOR SPECIAL EVENTS
AND PRIVATE PARTIES

713 366 2804 CELL
HILLERYPZ.BARTENDER@YAHOO.COM

MIXOLOGY 101

the
SIDECAR

1 1/2 oz. Brandy
1/2 oz. Triple Sec
1/2 oz. Lemon or Lime Juice

Combine all the ingredients
in a shaker filled with ice,
shake well and strain into a
cocktail glass.

MIXOLOGY 101

the
COSMOPOLITAN

1 1/2 oz. Vodka
1/2 oz. Cointreau or Triple Sec
3/4 oz. Lime Juice

Combine all the ingredients
in a cocktail shaker filled with
ice. Shake well. Strain into a
cocktail glass and garnish with
a lime squeeze.

MIXOLOGY 101

the
MANHATTAN

1 1/2 oz. Maker's Mark
Bourbon
1/4 oz. Sweet Vermouth or
Dry Vermouth
dash Angostura Bitters
(optional)

Combine all the ingredients
in a cocktail shaker filled with
ice. Shake well. Strain into a
cocktail glass and garnish
with a cherry.

Mas-Abajo
DRINK & FUN RESTAU

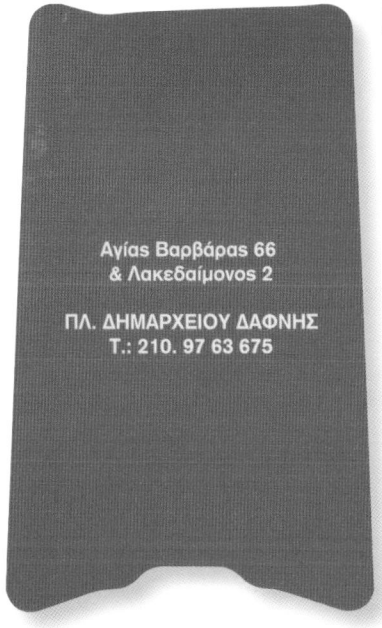
Αγίας Βαρβάρας 66
& Λακεδαίμονος 2
ΠΛ. ΔΗΜΑΡΧΕΙΟΥ ΔΑΦΝΗΣ
Τ.: 210. 97 63 675

2

e mail
fanipart@gmail.com

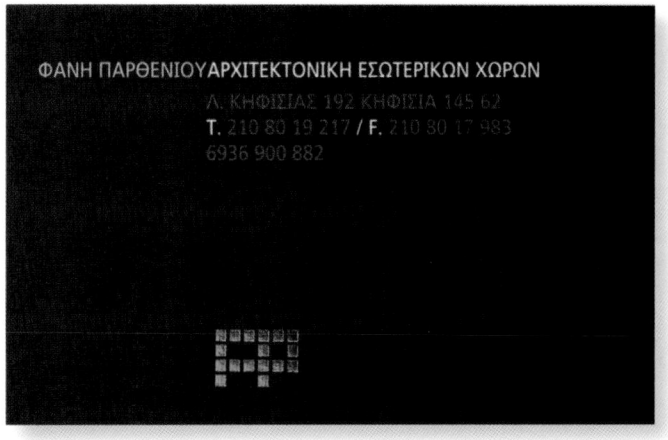
ΦΑΝΗ ΠΑΡΘΕΝΙΟΥ ΑΡΧΙΤΕΚΤΟΝΙΚΗ ΕΣΩΤΕΡΙΚΩΝ ΧΩΡΩΝ
Λ. ΚΗΦΙΣΙΑΣ 192 ΚΗΦΙΣΙΑ 145 62
Τ. 210 80 19 217 / F. 210 80 17 983
6936 900 882

3

joe masquelier
industrial designer
T 209.836.2078
C 209.814.6951
jmasquelier@gmail.com

1

joe masquelier
industrial designer
T 209.836.2078
C 209.814.6951
jmasquelier@gmail.com

joe masquelier
industrial designer
T 209.836.2078
C 209.814.6951
jmasquelier@gmail.com

the
sorrell
company
1106 SEMINARY PLACE RICHMOND VA 23227-5044
T: (804)627 0444 M: (804)405 6677
BILL@THESORRELLCOMPANY.COM WWW.THESORRELLCOMPANY.COM
bill sorrell
+ + + + + + + BRIGHT IDEAS TO GO

1

Se·man·tix
distinction for business and brands
Se·man·tix
office: 310.204.2004
fax: 310.204.4879
always: 310.433.5353
4445 overland avenue
culver city, ca 90230
Jamil Barrie
principal
brand strategist
copywriter
jbarrie@semantixcreative.com
www.semantixcreative.com

2

3

FEASTS of FANCY

PAIGE INMAN catering & event manager

THE HOBBS BUILDING
1427 WEST NINTH STREET · SUITE 103 · KANSAS CITY, MISSOURI 64101
phone 816.841.0166 · www.theweddingcafe.com

STYLISH FOOD & URBAN ELEGANCE

4

ALTER KLOSTERHOF
RESTAURANT

TOBIAS SCHNABEL
GASTGEBER

EBERSTÄDTER STRASSE 7
74182 OBERSULM/SÜLZBACH

TELEFON (071 34) 188 55
TELEFAX (071 34) 91 63 48

WWW.RESTAURANT-ALTER-KLOSTERHOF.DE
INFO@RESTAURANT-ALTER-KLOSTERHOF.DE

ÖFFNUNGSZEITEN
DIENSTAG – SAMSTAG

18.00 UHR – 24.00 UHR
UND NACH VEREINBARUNG

1

design firm: Lizette Gecel
designer: Lizette Gecel
client: The Sorrell Company
software/hardware: Adobe Illustrator CS2
paper/materials: Neenah Paper
Eames Furniture

2

design firm: Evenson Design
art director: Stan Evenson
designer: Mark Sojka
client: Semantix Creative
software/hardware: EPS

3

design firm: Bungalow Creative
art director: Christopher Huelshorst
designer: Carrie Kish
client: Feasts of Fancy
software/hardware: Quark Xpress
paper/materials: Carnival Vellum 100 lb cover

4

design firm: Jens Mogler
designer: Jens Mogler
client: Restaurant Alter Klosterhof
software/hardware: Macromedia Freehand
paper/materials: Gmund Blanc Beige Creme

1

ZACK FUENTES
Owner Operator
zfuentes@unclebillysaustin.com
1530 BARTON SPRINGS RD
AUSTIN, TEXAS 78704
unclebillysaustin.com
512.476.0100 TEL
512.476.0104 FAX

AUSTIN'S ORIGINAL
UNCLE
Billy's
BREW&QUE
QUALITY CRAFTED

SHANE STARK
Owner Operator
sstark@unclebillysaustin.com
1530 BARTON SPRINGS RD
AUSTIN, TEXAS 78704
unclebillysaustin.com
512.476.0100 TEL
512.476.0104 FAX

DARREN HARRELL
General Manager
dharrell@unclebillysaustin.com
1530 BARTON SPRINGS RD
AUSTIN, TEXAS 78704
unclebillysaustin.com
512.476.0100 TEL
512.476.0104 FAX

2

TOP OF THE LINE
BUILDERS
DESIGN • REMODEL • BUILD
CHRIS PAGANELLI
[510]407.1978
LICENSE # 853928

TOP OF THE LINE
BUILDERS
DESIGN • REMODEL • BUILD
TOPOFTHELINEBUILDERS.COM
4061 EAST CASTRO VALLEY BLVD #71 | CASTRO VALLEY, CA 94552

3

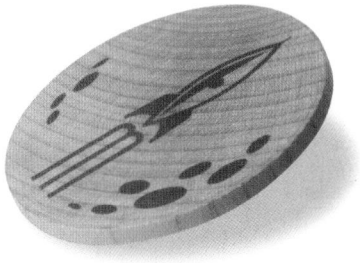

1

design firm: Idea 21
art director: Tom Berno
designer: Jeff Davis
client: Uncle Billy's: Brew and Que
software/hardware: Adobe CS2
paper/materials: Letterpress on coaster stock

2

design firm: Miles Design
art director: Josh Miles
designer: Eric Folzenlogel
client: Top of the Line Builders
software/hardware: Adobe Illustrator CS2
paper/materials: French Kraft 100 lb cover

3

design firm: Murillo Design, Inc.
art director: Roland Murillo
designer: Roland Murillo
client: Murillo Design, Inc.
paper/materials: Wood

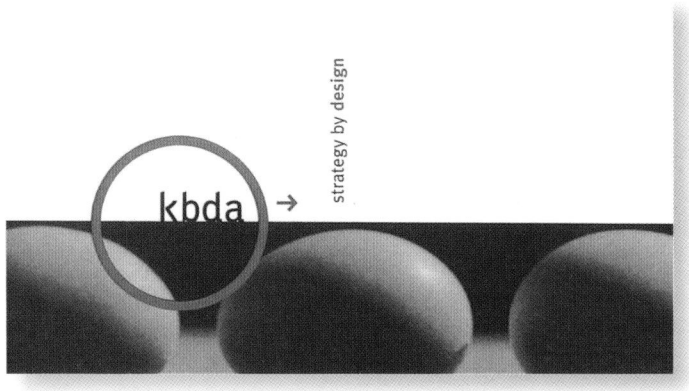
kbda
strategy by design

1
(p) 310.287.2400
(f) 310.287.0909
(w) kbda.com
2558 Overland Avenue
Los Angeles, CA 90064
kbda
Jamie Cavanaugh
New Media
jamiec@kbda.com

2
Ralph Deal
Composer, musician, engineer
161 Leverington Avenue,
Suite 1001,
Philadelphia, PA 19127-2034
215.483.2415 ph 215.483.4554 fx
audio-jack.com
Audio Jack
Purveyors of fine music & sound design
Audio Jack

57TH & IRVING
PRODUCTIONS

TOM GANJAMIE
Director of Development

645 Madison Avenue, Suite 9B
New York, New York 10022
phone: 212-995-0057 *cell:* 908-787-3090
email: tom@57irving.com *web:* www.57irving.com

3

marisa estrada
o)323.230.9600 c)323.252.9398 e)info@ritzyperiwinkle.com

ritzyperiwinkle.com

4

RITZY PERIWINKLE
fade proof design sweetness...

1

design firm: KBDA
art director: Kim Baer
designer: Jamie Diersing
client: KBDA
software/hardware: Adobe

2

design firm: D4 Creative Group
art director: Wicky Lee
client: Audio Jack
software/hardware: Adobe Photoshop and Quark Xpress
paper/materials: Strathmore Bright White

3

design firm: Matthew Schwartz Design Studio
art director: Matthew Schwartz
client: 57th and Irving Productions
software/hardware: Adobe Illustrator and InDesign

4

design firm: Ritzy Periwinkle
art director: Marisa Estrada
designer: Marisa Estrada
client: Ritzy Periwinkle
software/hardware: Adobe Illustrator
paper/materials: 2/2 Classic Crest Soft White Super Smooth

Sean Baker
Senior Designer

Liquid Agency | Brand Marketing
448 S. Market Street
San Jose, CA 95113
T 408.850.8859
M 510.329.7189
E sean@liquidagency.com
W liquidagency.com

liquid

Isalda (Izzy) Hermosillo
Accounting Specialist

Liquid Agency | Brand Marketing
448 S. Market Street
San Jose, CA 95113
T 408.850.8839
E izzy@liquidagency.com
W liquidagency.com

liquid

Julia Held
Designer

Liquid Agency | Brand Marketing
448 S. Market Street
San Jose, CA 95113
T 408.850.8849
M 408.209.5822
E julia@liquidagency.com
W liquidagency.com

liquid

1

2

3

1

design firm: Liquid Agency
art director: Alfredo Muccino
designer: Joshua Swanbeck
client: Liquid Agency
software/hardware: Adobe InDesign
paper/materials: Plastic

2

design firm: Geyrhalter Design
art director: Fabian Geyrhalter
designer: Fabian Geyrhalter and Jacqueline Sung
client: Fabian Geyrhalter Photography
software/hardware: Adobe Illustrator
paper/materials: Plastic

3

design firm: Eyebeam Creative LLC
art director: Greg Gersch
designer: Greg Gersch
client: Eyebeam Creative LLC
software/hardware: Adobe Illustrator and Quark Xpress
paper/materials: Strathmore Ultimate White Laid 110 lb cover

1

O's
DAVID GARRIDO
O's Campus Cafe and Catering
ACES Building
201 East 24th Street 2.234
Austin, Texas 78712-2.234
phone: (512) 232-9060
fax: (512) 232-9097
email: ocafe@mail.aces.utexas.edu
web: www.aces.utexas.edu/ocafe

CAMPUS CAFE

O's

2

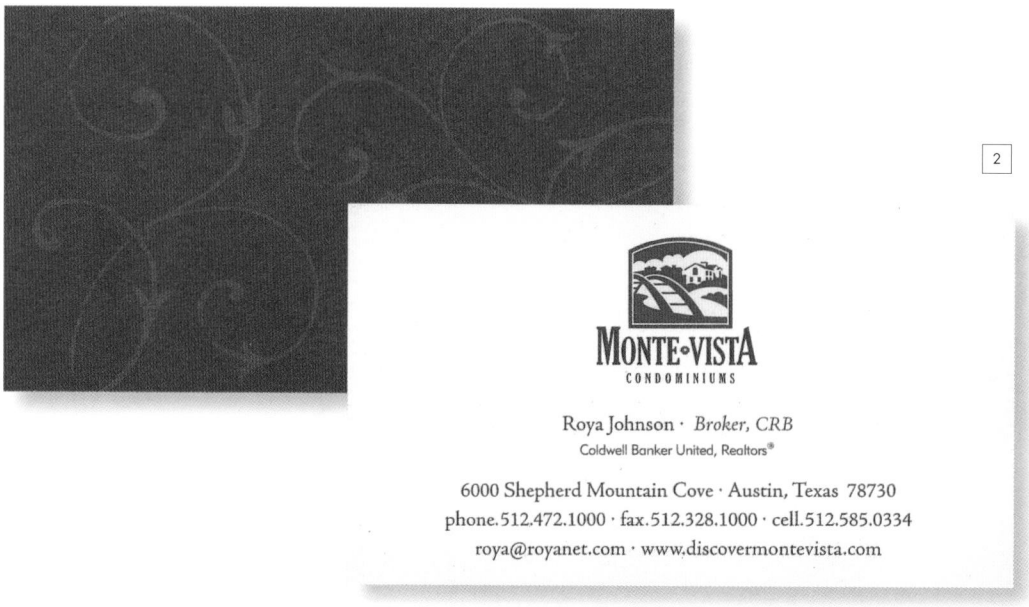
MONTE•VISTA
CONDOMINIUMS
Roya Johnson · Broker, CRB
Coldwell Banker United, Realtors®
6000 Shepherd Mountain Cove · Austin, Texas 78730
phone.512.472.1000 · fax.512.328.1000 · cell.512.585.0334
roya@royanet.com · www.discovermontevista.com

3

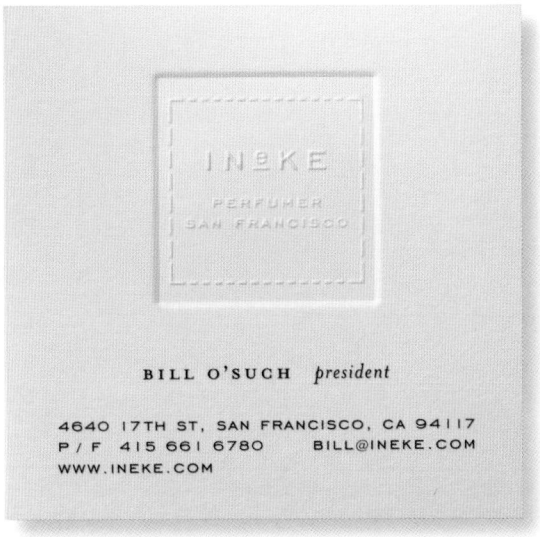

4

1

design firm: Sibley Peteet Design—Austin
art director: Rex Peteet
designer: Rex Peteet
client: O's Campus Cafe
software/hardware: Adobe InDesign and Quark Xpress
paper/materials: Card stock with fleck

2

design firm: Sibley Peteet Design—Austin
art director: Rex Peteet
designer: Kris Worley
client: Monte Vista Condominiums
software/hardware: Adobe InDesign and Quark Xpress
paper/materials: Via Felt

3

design firm: Helena Seo Design
art director: Helena Seo
designer: Helena Seo
client: Ineke, LLC
software/hardware: Adobe Illustrator

4

design firm: smashLAB
art director: Eric Karjaluoto
designer: Peter Pimentel
illustrator: Peter Pimentel
client: The Northern BC Tourism Association
software/hardware: Adobe Illustrator
paper/materials: Cougar Cover 100 lb cover

1

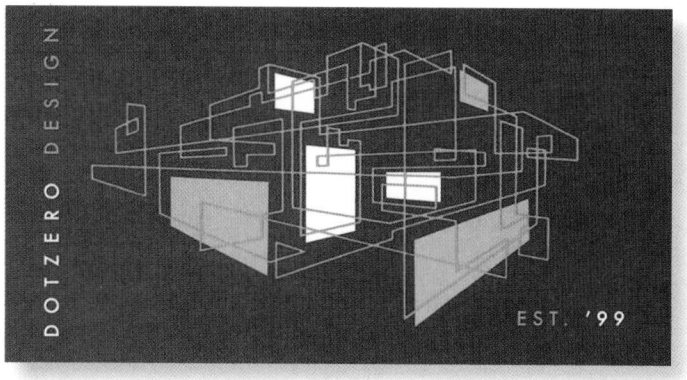
DOTZERO DESIGN
EST. '99

KAREN WIPPICH
208 SW STARK ST, #307 • PORTLAND, OR 97204
tel: 503 892 9262 fax: 503 228 9403
email: karenw@dotzerodesign.com www.dotzerodesign.com

(karen wippich)
karenw@dotzerodesign.com
503.892.9262 TEL
503.228.9403 FAX
208 SW Stark St, #307
Portland, Oregon 97204
www.dotzerodesign.com
dotzero design

DOTZERO DESIGN
www.dotzerodesign.com

Karen Wippich karenw@dotzerodesign.com
208 SW Stark St // #307 // Portland, OR 97204
PH: [503] 892 9262 // FX: [503] 228 9403
www.dotzerodesign.com

Dotzero

2

3

1

design firm: Dotzero Design
designer: Karen Wippich and Jon Wippich
client: Dotzero Design
software/hardware: Adobe Illustrator and Photoshop
paper/materials: Neenah Eames Furniture

2

design firm: Timber Design Co.
art director: Lars Lawson
client: Timber Design Co.
software/hardware: Freehand and Quark Xpress
paper/materials: Starwhite Tiara Vellum

3

design firm: Blok
art director: Vanessa Eckstein
designer: Vanessa Eckstein
client: Bandolero Films
software/hardware: Adobe Illustrator

1

Johnston
DUFFY
www.johnstonduffy.com
Johnston
DUFFY
MARTIN DUFFY
martin@johnstonduffy.com PHONE 215 389 2888 FAX 215 389 2988
803 S°4TH STREET First Floor PHILADELPHIA PENNSYLVANIA 19147 3103

2

Sasha's
suds n duds
Sasha's
suds n duds
a self service dog wash and pet boutique
Jan Bulawa
jan@sashassudsnduds.com
2418 B Sunset Blvd.
Houston, Texas 77055
713.533.1117
www.sashassudsnduds.com

3

Nettables
delectable accessories

Danette Miller

netteables@netteables.com
4647 E Chandler Blvd Suite #2
Phoenix, AZ 85048
p 480.705.0747 f 480.705.9626

netteables.com

4

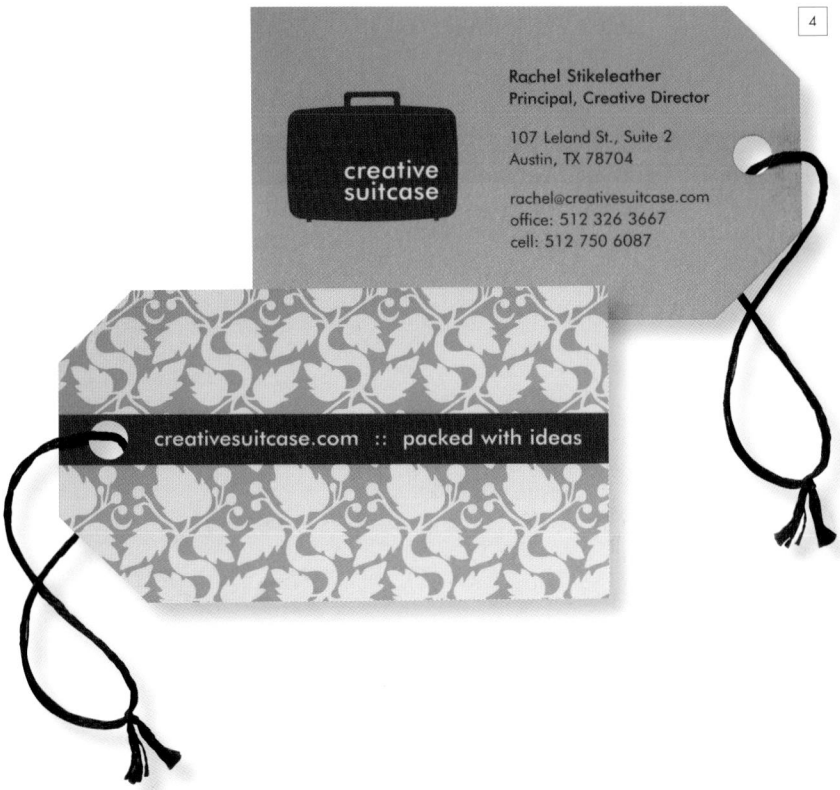

1

design firm: Johnston Duffy
art director: Martin Duffy
designer: Johnston Duffy
client: Johnston Duffy
software/hardware: Adobe Illustrator on MAC
paper/materials: Mohawk Superfine

2

design firm: Limb Design
art director: Linda Limb
designer: Trisha Cano
client: Shasha's Suds n Duds
software/hardware: Adobe InDesign

3

design firm: Campbell Fisher Design
art director: Greg Fisher
designer: Kristy Roehrs
client: Nettables (delectable accessories)
software/hardware: Adobe Illustrator
paper/materials: Domtar Carrara White 120 lb cover

4

design firm: Creative Suitcase
art director: Rachel Stikeleather
designer: Rachel Stikeleather
client: Creative Suitcase
software/hardware: Quark Xpress
paper/materials: Classic Crest

1

Ghada Ghanem | : SOPRANO
telephone **961.3.939141** : | ghadaghanem@yahoo.com

telephone **961.3.939141** : | ghadaghanem@yahoo.com

2

PÄGLIŪCO

PAGLIUCO DESIGN COMPANY
213 West Institute Place Suite 508 Chicago, Illinois 60610
T/312 943 4281 F/312 943 6946 W/ pagliuco.com

Michael Pagliuco / Principal
michael@pagliuco.com

3

elma backman
designer
m: elmaback@gmail.com
p: +354. 695 6900

4

1

design firm: Mayda Freije Makdessi
art director: Mayda Freije Makdessi
designer: Mayda Freije Makdessi
client: Ghada Ghanem
software/hardware: Adobe Illustrator and Quark Xpress
paper/materials: uncoated 200 gsm

2

design firm: Pagliuco Design Company
art director: Michael Pagliuco
designer: Michael Pagliuco
client: Pagliuco Design Company
paper/materials: Mohawk Superfine

3

design firm: Nicole Nicolaus
art director: Nicole Nicolaus
designer: Nicole Nicolaus
client: Elma Backman (fashion designer)
software/hardware: Adobe Illustrator and InDesign CS2
paper/materials: packaging paper, offset print

4

design firm: James Song
art director: James Song
designer: James Song
illustrator: James Song
client: James Song
software/hardware: Adobe Illustrator
paper/materials: Blind emboss on 110 lb matte paper

1

GARDENS
EXTRAORDINARY WORKS INSIDE AND OUT
1818 WEST 35TH AUSTIN, TEXAS 78703
PHONE: 512.451.5490 FAX: 512.451.4523

2

EMPRESS

Ardi Entezam
8264 Sunset Boulevard
West Hollywood, California 90046
323-656-8377 T
323-656-8457 F
ardi@empressrestaurant.com
empressrestaurant.com

3

JULIE GRANTZ
LISTEN : SENTIRE
87 LINDA AVENUE, PIEDMONT, CA 94611
JULIE@JULIEGRANTZ.COM 510.290.4579

DENHERDERDESIGN
graphic design | illustration
T № 231 590 3583
E jesse@denherderdesign.com
Jesse DenHerder

DENHERDERDESIGN
graphic design | illustration
RETURN ▶
PO BOX
№ 324
CENTRAL LAKE, MI
49622
denherderdesign.com

1

THE OUTFIT
MEDIA GROUP
DONN J. VIOLA
CREATIVE DIRECTOR, PARTNER
FULL SERVICE PRODUCTION COMPANY • WWW.THEOUTFITMG.COM
310-571-2370
CELL 323-741-7066
FAX 310-571-2376
DJ@THEOUTFITMG.COM
2038 ARMACOST AVENUE 2ND FLOOR
LOS ANGELES, CA 90025-6113

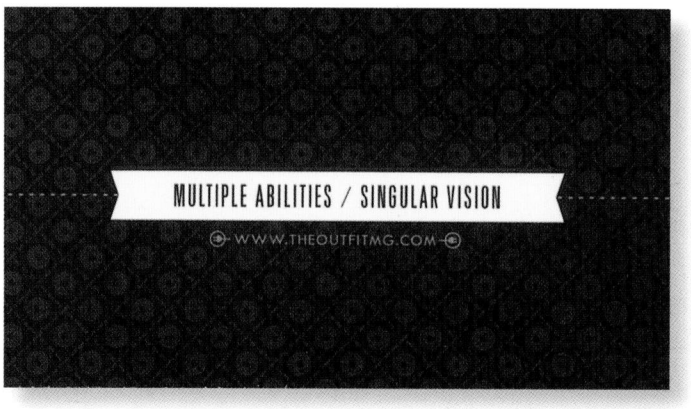
MULTIPLE ABILITIES / SINGULAR VISION
WWW.THEOUTFITMG.COM

2

3

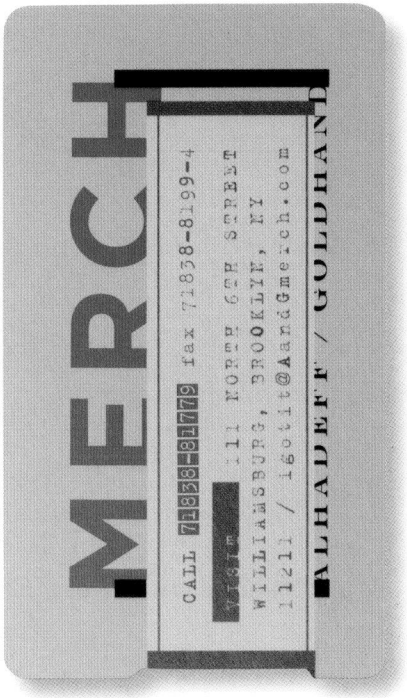

4

1

design firm: Den Herder Design
art director: Jesse Den Herder
designer: Jesser Den Herder
illustrator: Jesse Den Herder
client: Den Herder Design
software/hardware: Adobe Illustrator CS, Adobe Photoshop CS

2

design firm: The Decoder Ring Design Concern
designer: Christian Helms
client: The Outfit Media Group
software/hardware: Adobe Illustrator
paper/materials: Cougar Opaque

3

design firm: Nothing: Something: NY
art director: Kevin Landwehr
designer: Kevin Landwehr and Devin Becker
client: The Alembic Bar & Restaurant
paper/materials: Neenah Classic Crest Natural White 130 lb

4

design firm: Nothing: Something: NY
art director: Kevin Landwehr

1

www.unicorntheatre.org

CYNTHIA LEVIN
Producing Artistic Director
P 816.531.7529 x11 • F 816.531.0421
clevin@unicorntheatre.org
UNICORN
THEATRE
3828 MAIN STREET
KANSAS CITY, MO 64111

2

BWMGROUP
PHILIP WANKE ASLA
PRINCIPAL
T : [512] 238 8912
F : [512] 238 8913
E : pwanke@bwmgrp.com
bwmgrp.com
102 E. MAIN, SUITE 200, ROUND ROCK, TX 78664

3

FORTNER·HALL
ARTISAN TEXTILES
Ames Hall Master Weaver
1706 Wyandotte • Kansas City, Missouri 64108
phone 816.210.4711 • fax 816.421.8750

1

bungalow

bungalowCREATIVE
Carrie Kish
carrie@bungalowcreative.com
ph: 816.421.8770 fax: 816.421.8750
www.bungalowcreative.com
1919 Wyandotte
Kansas City, MO 64108

bungalowCREATIVE
Christopher Huelshorst
christopher@bungalowcreative.com
ph: 816.421.8770 fax: 816.421.8750
www.bungalowcreative.com
1919 Wyandotte
Kansas City, MO 64108

bungalowCREATIVE
Christopher Huelshorst
christopher@bungalowcreative.com
ph: 816.421.8770 fax: 816.421.8750
www.bungalowcreative.com
1919 Wyandotte
Kansas City, MO 64108

2

Web Site Design
Graphic Design
Internet Marketing
Search Engine Optimization
Scott Allen
Web Design Consultant
949.310.3138
scott@hybrid6.com
www.hybrid6.com
H6 Hybrid6Studios

DONT
WALK
WALK
www.hybrid6.com

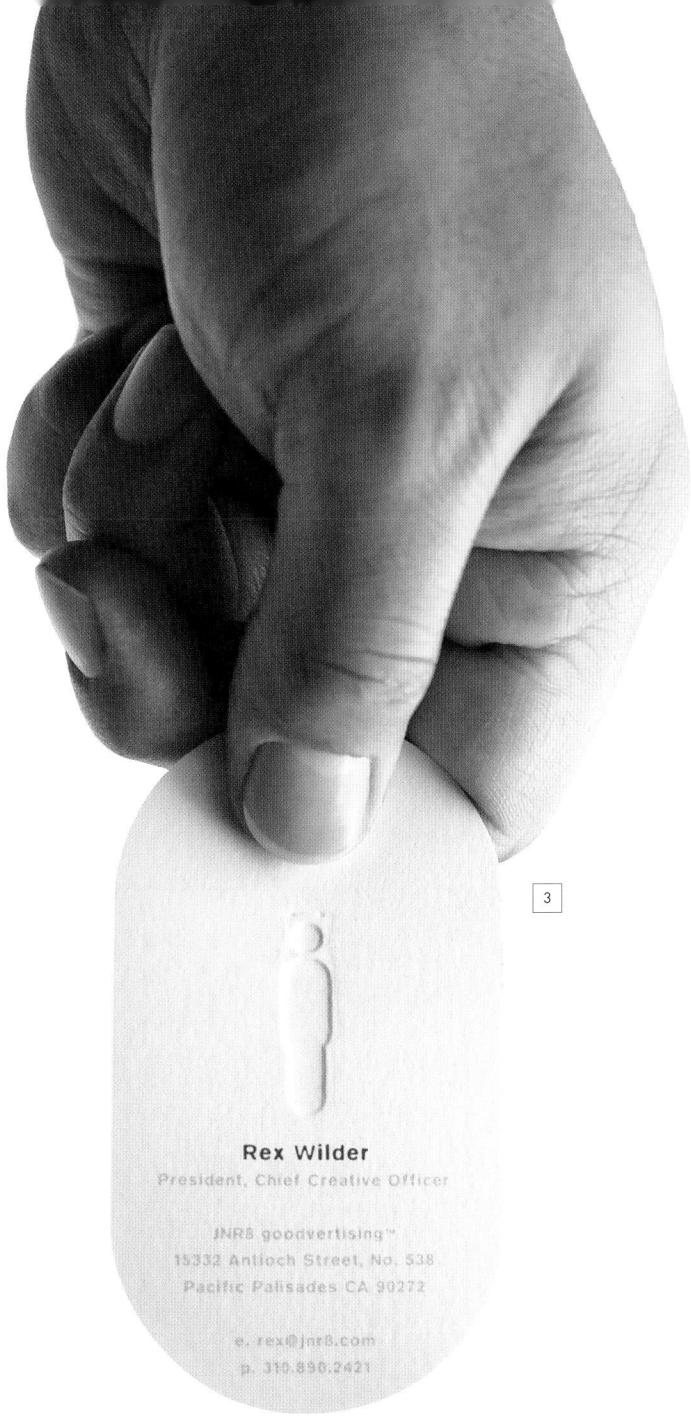
Rex Wilder
President, Chief Creative Officer
JNR8 goodvertising™
15332 Antioch Street, No. 538
Pacific Palisades CA 90272
e. rex@jnr8.com
p. 310.890.2421

3

1

Heather Beckel Guntert, Managing Director

I&O Communications
327 Congress, Suite 200 Austin, Texas 78701
heather@iandocom.com www.iandocom.com
p 512.288.4054 m 512.507.3809

io

insight & outreach

io

2

A DIVISION OF APOGEE DESIGNS

101 South Kane Street
Baltimore, MD 21224
www.hardguard.com

P 410 633 6336 x 28
F 410 633 3666
C 443 744 0370

HARDGUARD®

KEVIN BARNES
VICE PRESIDENT, PRODUCT DEVELOPMENT
kevin.barnes@apogeedesigns.com

Chase Wilson
CF-24

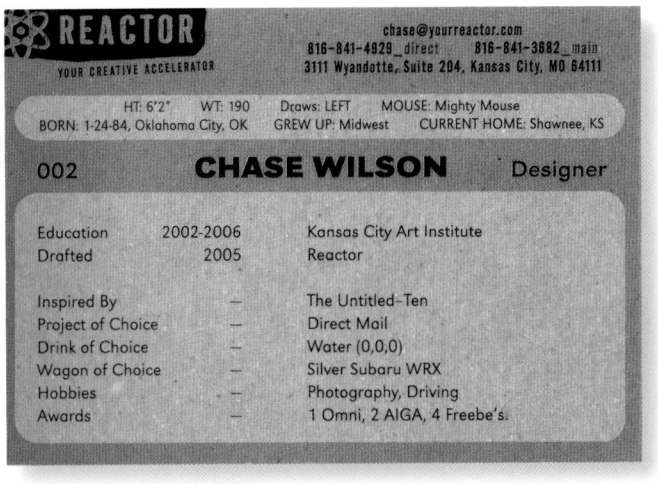
REACTOR
YOUR CREATIVE ACCELERATOR
chase@yourreactor.com
816-841-4929_direct 816-841-3682_main
3111 Wyandotte, Suite 204, Kansas City, MO 64111
HT: 6'2" WT: 190 Draws: LEFT MOUSE: Mighty Mouse
BORN: 1-24-84, Oklahoma City, OK GREW UP: Midwest CURRENT HOME: Shawnee, KS
002 CHASE WILSON Designer
Education 2002-2006 Kansas City Art Institute
Drafted 2005 Reactor
Inspired By — The Untitled-Ten
Project of Choice — Direct Mail
Drink of Choice — Water (0,0,0)
Wagon of Choice — Silver Subaru WRX
Hobbies — Photography, Driving
Awards — 1 Omni, 2 AIGA, 4 Freebe's.

3

1B-8
REACTOR
Clifton Alexander

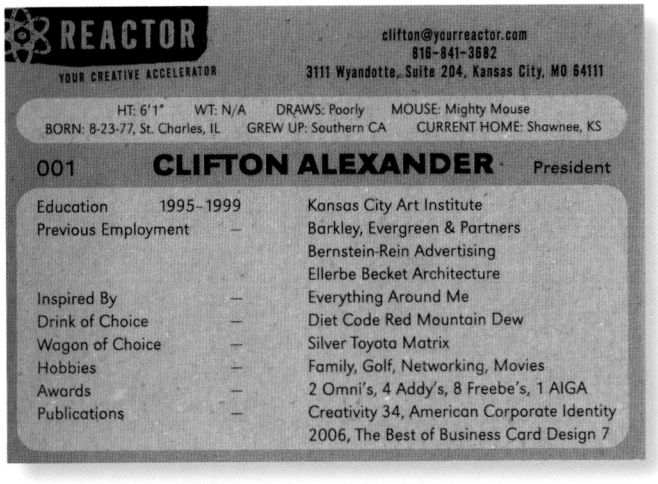
REACTOR
YOUR CREATIVE ACCELERATOR
clifton@yourreactor.com
816-841-3682
3111 Wyandotte, Suite 204, Kansas City, MO 64111
HT: 6'1" WT: N/A DRAWS: Poorly MOUSE: Mighty Mouse
BORN: 8-23-77, St. Charles, IL GREW UP: Southern CA CURRENT HOME: Shawnee, KS
001 CLIFTON ALEXANDER President
Education 1995-1999 Kansas City Art Institute
Previous Employment — Barkley, Evergreen & Partners
Bernstein-Rein Advertising
Ellerbe Becket Architecture
Inspired By — Everything Around Me
Drink of Choice — Diet Code Red Mountain Dew
Wagon of Choice — Silver Toyota Matrix
Hobbies — Family, Golf, Networking, Movies
Awards — 2 Omni's, 4 Addy's, 8 Freebe's, 1 AIGA
Publications — Creativity 34, American Corporate Identity
2006, The Best of Business Card Design 7

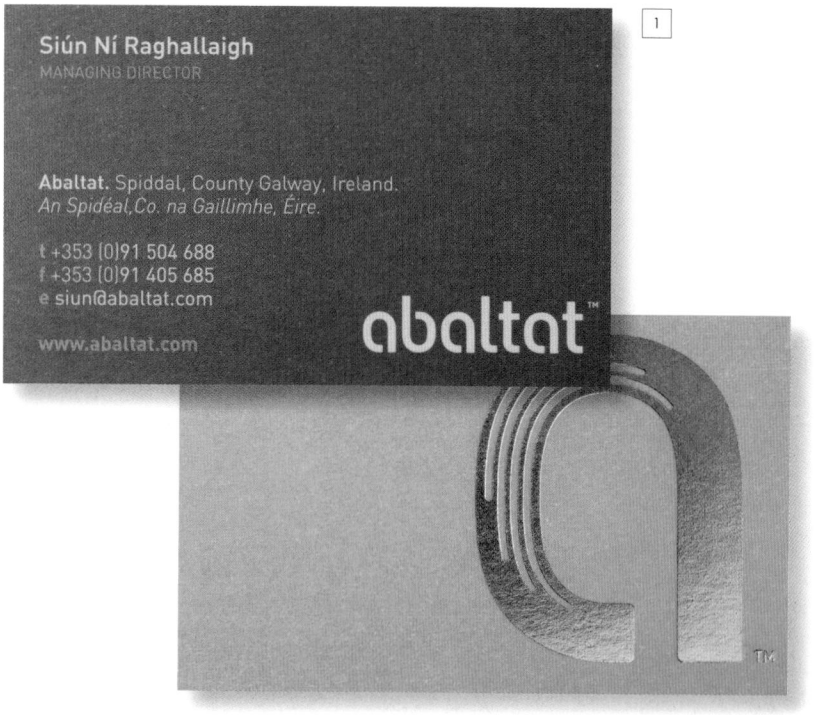
Siún Ní Raghallaigh
MANAGING DIRECTOR
Abaltat. Spiddal, County Galway, Ireland.
An Spidéal, Co. na Gaillimhe, Éire.
t +353 (0)91 504 688
f +353 (0)91 405 685
e siun@abaltat.com
www.abaltat.com
abaltat™
TM

1

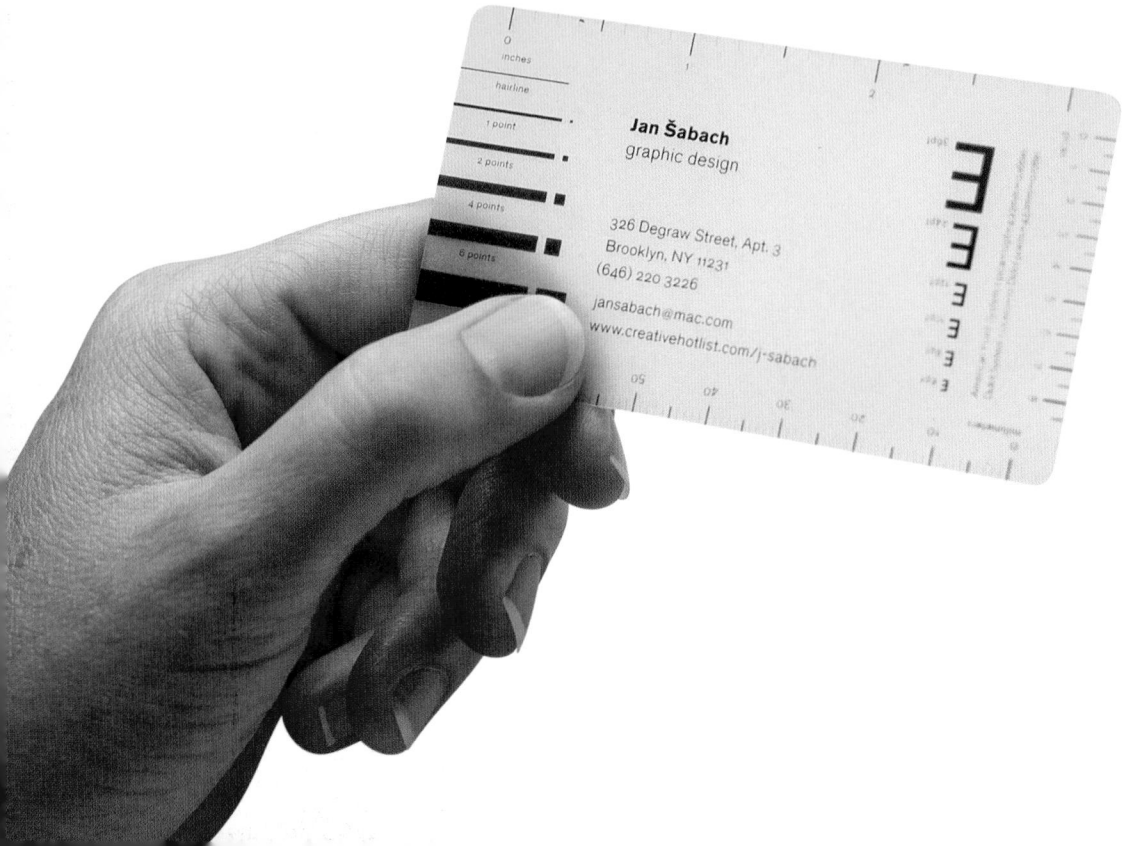
Jan Šabach
graphic design
326 Degraw Street, Apt. 3
Brooklyn, NY 11231
(646) 220 3226
jansabach@mac.com
www.creativehotlist.com/j-sabach

2

3

4

1

design firm: Detail Design Studio
art director: Detail Design Studio
designer: Detail Design Studio
client: Abaltat
software/hardware: Adobe Illustrator and InDesign
paper/materials: Arcoprint

2

design firm: Jan Šabach Design
art director: Jan Šabach
designer: Jan Šabach
client: Jan Šabach
software/hardware: Adobe InDesign

3

design firm: Lolight Design
art director: Aaron Deckler
designer: Aaron Deckler
client: ezGDS Inc.
software/hardware: Adobe Illustrator and InDesign
paper/materials: Cougar 100 lb

4

design firm: Johnston Duffy
art director: Martin Duffy
designer: Martin Duffy and Chris Johnston
client: Tag Communication Services
software/hardware: Adobe Illustrator on MAC
paper/materials: Die-cut with string

1

LEFTY
Lefty Lexington
{ design }

John Rockwell
{by Nate Garn}
Nate Garn
{by John Rockwell}
NATE GARN
608 205 2067
www.LEFTYLEXINGTON.com

Lefty Lexington
{ design }

2

3

4

1

design firm: Lefty Lexington Design
art director: Nate Garn and John Rockwell
designer: Nate Garn and John Rockwell
client: Lefty Lexington Design
software/hardware: Adobe Photoshop and Quark Xpress
paper/materials: French

2

design firm: The Decoder Ring Design Concern
designer: Derrit DeRouen
client: DeRouen & Company
software/hardware: Adobe Photoshop
paper/materials: Gmund Sandstone

3

design firm: Evenson Design
art director: Stan Evenson
designer: Mark Sojka
client: Waldorf Crawford
software/hardware: EPS

4

design firm: Boxwood Press
art director: Cheryl L. Clark
designer: Cheryl L. Clark
illustrator: Cheryl L. Clark
client: Boxwood Press
paper/materials: Rives BFK

bluebird
CAFE

TWEET! TWEET! EAT!
LUNCH - MONDAY - FRIDAY
DINNER - THURSDAY - SATURDAY
BRUNCH - SATURDAY + SUNDAY
1700 SUMMIT
KANSAS CITY MISSOURI
816-221-7559

1

ROSEHIP
FLORA
Erin Knipp 512.917.6513
erin@rosehipflora.com
www.rosehipflora.com

3

Hill Country Weavers
South Congress Austin, Texas 78704
512 707 7396
www.hillcountryweavers.com
info@hillcountryweavers.com
Hill Country Weavers
South Congress Austin, Texas 78704
512 707 7396
www.hillcountryweavers.com
suzanne@hillcountryweavers.com
Hill Country Weavers
South Congress Austin, Texas 78704
512 707 7396
www.hillcountryweavers.com
info@hillcountryweavers.com

2

1

AVENELLE ARCHILLE

Belles Pralines

new orleans, louisiana
PHONE 504.952.2631
WEB www.bellespralines.com

2

3

Bakken
creative co.
801 Clay St. Oakland
California 94607
P: 510.452.8200
F: 510.452.0934
bakkencreativeco.com

Your name is? Michelle Bakken
Your job title is? Creative director
Your claim to fame? Embellishings
where to reach you? mbakken@bakkencreativeco.com

Bakken
creative co.
801 Clay St. Oakland
California 94607
P: 510.452.8200
F: 510.452.0934
bakkencreativeco.com

Who are you? Michelle Bakken
Your forte? Creative director
One of your recent brilliant ideas? mandatory field trips
your email? mbakken@bakkencreativeco.com

Bakken
creative co.
801 Clay St. Oakland
California 94607
P: 510.452.8200
F: 510.452.0934
bakkencreativeco.com

What do you go by? Michelle Bakken
What's your craft? Creative director
Where do you find inspiration? looking through a camera
contact info? mbakken@bakkencreativeco.com

1

PRISM

Jon K. Rodgers
Principal

Prism Development Company
625 N Michigan Avenue Suite 500
Chicago Illinois 60611
P 312 782 6700
F 312 782 6401
j.rodgers@prismcompany.com
prismcompany.com

2

SUSAN SMELTZER

ESTEEMED CONCERT PIANIST, COMPOSER, AND TEACHER *extraordinaire* of over 25 years: US representative to the Second Van Cliburn International Piano Competition and recipient of the 1969 Fulbright Scholarship to Vienna • PRIVATE LESSONS for students of *all ages*

713 991 4945

8102 Tavenor Lane, Houston, Texas 77075

3

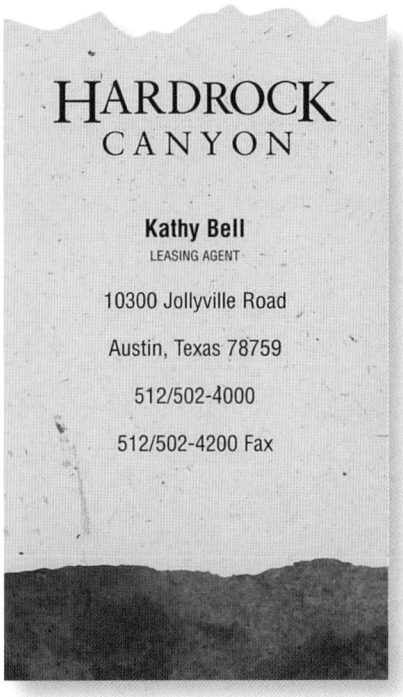

4

1

design firm: Pagliuco Design Company
art director: Michael Pagliuco
designer: Michael Pagliuco
client: Prism Development Compa
paper/materials: Mohawk Superfine

2

design firm: Ingeniosus Studios, Inc.
art director: Caspar Lam
designer: Caspar Lam
client: Susan Smeltzer
software/hardware: Adobe InDesign
paper/materials: Uncoated 100 lb cover

3

design firm: Pinpoint Communications
art director: James Kluetz
designer: Paul Cooper
client: Elite Getaways
software/hardware: Adobe Illustrator and InDesign CS
paper/materials: Classic Crest Solar White 130 lb DTC

4

design firm: Haute Haus Creative
art director: Don Lewis
designer: Don Lewis
client: Hardrock Canyon
software/hardware: Freehand/ Quark Xpress
paper/materials: French Speckletone

1

SUBPLOT DESIGN INC.
The Mercantile Building, 318 Homer Street, Suite 301
Vancouver, British Columbia, Canada V6B 2V2
Telephone 604 685 2990 Facsimile 604 685 2909
www.subplot.com
SUBPLOT
MATTHEW CLARK
Direct 778 893 0412
matthew@subplot.com
SUBPLOT DESIGN INC.
The Mercantile Building, 318 Homer Street, Suite 301
Vancouver, British Columbia, Canada V6B 2V2
Telephone 604 685 2990 Facsimile 604 685 2909
www.subplot.com
ROY WHITE
Direct 778 893 0422
roy@subplot.com
SUBPLOT

2

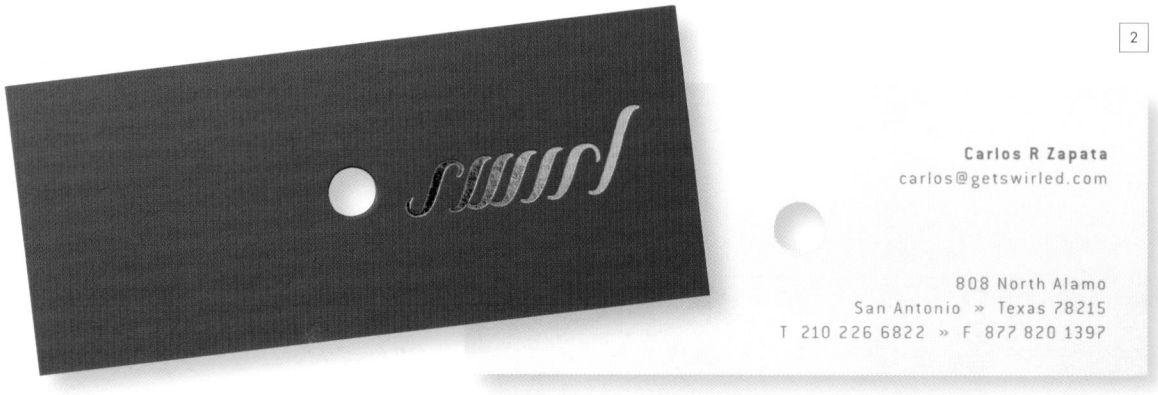
swirl
Carlos R Zapata
carlos@getswirled.com
808 North Alamo
San Antonio » Texas 78215
T 210 226 6822 » F 877 820 1397

3

1

design firm: Subplot Design, Inc.
art director: Matthew Clark and Roy White
designer: Matthew Clark and Roy White
client: Subplot Design, Inc.
software/hardware: Adobe Illustrator
paper/materials: Pegasus Supersmooth and Hand-tipped labels

2

design firm: Swirl
designer: Carlos R. Zapata
client: Swirl
software/hardware: Adobe Illustrator and InDesign CS2
paper/materials: Neenah Paper, Classic Columns, Duplex Cover—Red Pepper/So-

3

design firm: Flipcide
art director: Roy Dequina
designer: Roy Dequina and Pavla Diab
client: Flipcide
software/hardware: Adobe Illustrator
paper/materials: Fox River Sirius 130 lb cover

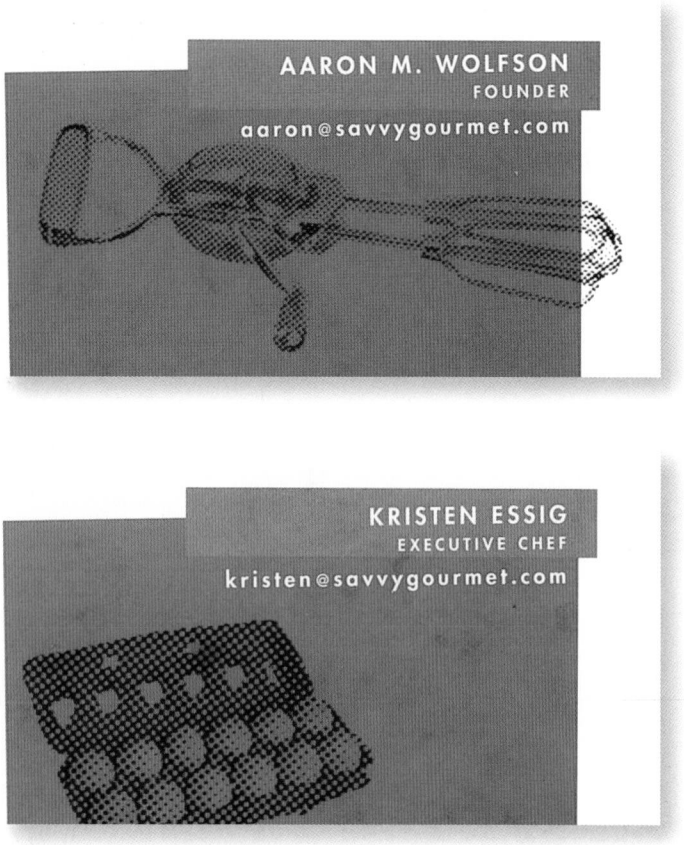
AARON M. WOLFSON
FOUNDER
aaron@savvygourmet.com
KRISTEN ESSIG
EXECUTIVE CHEF
kristen@savvygourmet.com

CLASSES | COOKWARE | CATERING
THE SAVVY GOURMET
4519 MAGAZINE ST. 70115
NEW ORLEANS
N.O.LA
EAT IT UP!
COOK
504 895 2665 TEL
895 2664 FAX
WWW.SAVVYGOURMET.COM

1

BRADLEY T. LYNCH 312.805.0505 bl@brininstool-lynch.com

2

3

4

1

design firm: Zande + Newman Design
art director: Adam Newman
designer: Adam Newman
client: The Savvy Gourmet
software/hardware: Adobe Illustrator
paper/materials: French Durotone

2

design firm: Liska + Associates
art director: Steve Liska
designer: Tantika Tivorat
client: Brad Lynch
software/hardware: Adobe InDesign and Illustrator
paper/materials: Crane's Kid Finish
Flourescent White 179 lb cover

3

design firm: smashLAB
art director: Eric Karjaluoto
designer: Peter Pimentel
client: Sinkit
software/hardware: Adobe Illustrator
paper/materials: Glama clear cover

4

design firm: Paragon Marketing Communications
art director: Louai Alasfahani
designer: Khalid Al-Rifae
client: Paragon Marketing Communications
software/hardware: Adobe Illustrator
paper/materials: Fedrigoni 20 gsm

1

2

1

design firm: Sheriff Design
art director: Paul Sheriff
designer: Paul Sheriff
client: Towers and Turrets

2

design firm: CDI Studios
art director: Brian Felgar
designer: Tracy Casstevens
client: Three Square

3

design firm: Briedis
art director: Ruuta Birina
designer: Ruuta Birina
client: R.B. Bairin

3

ANNO
FRISK FLØDE
BUSINESS CARD
100%

R.B.Bairin
+ 371 639 46 47
bairin[at]gmail.com
ruutabirina

1

nu
novia
UNDERWRITERS
JOHN R. RETZ
EXECUTIVE VICE PRESIDENT
JRETZ@NOVIA-UNDERWRITERS.COM
W : 317.791.6684 EXT. 223
F : 317.791.6680
NOVIA UNDERWRITERS, INC.
nu
503 EAST NATIONAL AVENUE INDIANAPOLIS, IN 46227 - 1246
WWW.NOVIA-UNDERWRITERS.COM

2

YIELD
scott murray
president & ceo
p 512.450.5150
m 512.762.9645
f 512.391.1782
scott.murray@yieldinc.com
823 congress avenue
suite 525
austin, texas 78701
www.yieldinc.com

3

Bill Zbaren
photographer

ZBAREN

2232 West Giddings Street
Chicago, Illinois 60625
773 218 9395
bz@zbaren.com

4

705, RUE GOHIER, MONTRÉAL (QUÉBEC) H4L 3H9
514.744.6311
DOMINIQUE@LAMBERTCOMMUNICATIONS.COM
WWW.LAMBERTCOMMUNICATIONS.COM

DOMINIQUE LAMBERT
COMMUNICATIONS + RELATIONS PUBLIQUES

1

design firm: Miles Design
art director: Josh Miles
designer: Eric Folzenlogel
client: Novia
software/hardware: Adobe Illustrator CS
paper/materials: 100 lb cover, offset, emboss

2

design firm: MBA
art director: Mark Brinkman
designer: Caroline Pledger
client: Yield
software/hardware: Adobe Creative Suite
paper/materials: Strathmore Platinum White

3

design firm: Liska + Associates
art director: Steve Liska
designer: Vanessa Oltmanns
client: Bill Zbaren
software/hardware: Adobe InDesign and Illustrator
paper/materials: Mohawk Superfine 130 lb cover

4

design firm: Philippe Archontakis
art director: Philippe Archontakis

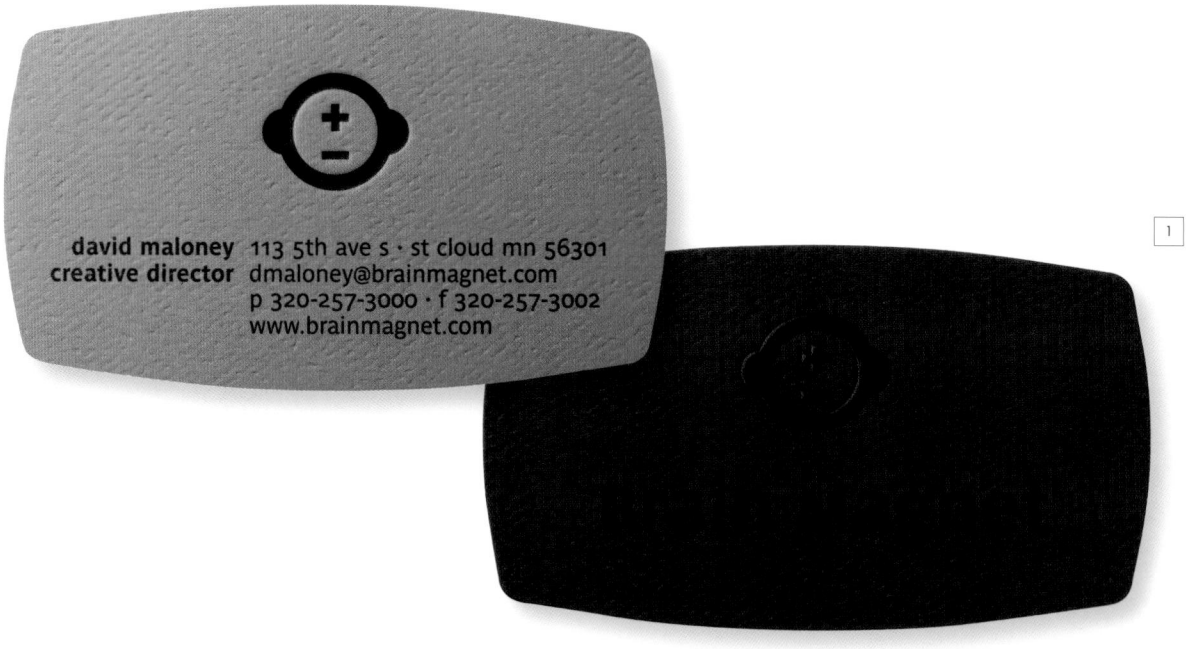
david maloney
creative director
113 5th ave s · st cloud mn 56301
dmaloney@brainmagnet.com
p 320-257-3000 · f 320-257-3002
www.brainmagnet.com

1

bt
bt architecture-energie
www.btae.ca
Jean Tardif
ARCHITECTE
T 514.578.9359
jtardif@btae.ca

2

www.steinzeit-mediendesign.de

steinzeit-mediendesign Ottweilerstraße 26a D-40476 Düsseldorf Fon: +49 211.48 46 84-0 Fax: +49 211.48 46 84-26 mail@steinzeit-mediendesign.de

3

STEIN ZEIT

steinzeit-mediendesign Ottweilerstraße 26a D-40476 Düsseldorf Fon: +49 211.48 46 84-0 Fax: +49 211.48 46 84-26 mail@steinzeit-mediendesign.de

360° Panorama-, HDR- & Objektfotografie

Designkonzepte für Print & Web

steinzeit-mediendesign

Peggy Stein
Diplom Designerin

Ottweilerstraße 26a
40476 Düsseldorf
Deutschland

Fon: +49 211.48 46 84-27
Fax: +49 211.48 46 84-26
Funk: +49 177.654 16 20

stein@steinzeit-mediendesign.de

THE HENLEY COLLEGE LIBRARY

1

1

design firm: Sagmeister Inc.
art director: Stefan Sagmeister
designer: Matthias Ernstberger
client: Sagmeister Inc.
software/hardware: Adobe Creative Suite

Matthias@ Sagmeister.com
222 West 14th Street, Suite 15A
New York City, NY 10011
T 212·647 1789 F 212·647 1788
www.Sagmeister.com

PAPER TOWER
STUDIOS
BROCK HENDERSON
847-513-2063
papertowerstudios.com
brock@papertowerstudios.com

1
PAPER TOWER
STUDIOS
BROCK HENDERSON
847-513-2063
papertowerstudios.com
brock@papertowerstudios.com

2
draw
A VIDEO PRODUCTION COMPANY
JOHN WARD / VIDEOGRAPHER
386 WEST 1ST AVENUE
COLUMBUS, OHIO 43201
P: 614.299.2660
E: JOHN@DRAWPRODUCTIONS.COM
WWW.DRAWPRODUCTIONS.COM

3

Jamie Gibbs - Director

Limited Fashion, 54 Bury Old Road,
Whitefield, Manchester, M45 6TL

Mob: 07739 710899 Tel: 0161 773 1038
Website: www.limitedfashion.co.uk
E-mail: jamie@limitedfashion.co.uk

4

SANDRA FRÆNKEL

CONSULTING
COACHING
COMMUNICATION

INNOVATIONSMANAGERIN/IHK
YORCKSTRASSE 22 65195 WIESBADEN
T 06 11-24 00 944 M 01 51-14 70 48 53
SF@SANDRA-FRAENKEL.COM

SANDRA FRÆNKEL

1

design firm: Paper Tower Studios
art director: Brock Henderson
designer: Brenden Jones
illustrator: Brenden Jones
client: Paper Tower Studios
software/hardware: Adobe Illustrator
paper/materials: Classic Crest Solar White 100 lb cover

2

design firm: Element
art director: Megan Graham
designer: Megan Graham
client: Draw Productions
software/hardware: Adobe InDesign

3

design firm: Creative Spark
art director: Neil Marra
designer: Andy Mallalieu
client: Limited Fashion
software/hardware: Adobe Illustrator
paper/materials: 300 gsm, matte laminated, spot varnished, day-glow pink

4

design firm: R975
art director: Marcel Kummerer
designer: Marcel Kummerer
client: Sandra Fraenkel
paper/materials: Splendorgel

1

consulting + development
for creative service firms
pound
interactive
jeremy pound
jeremy@poundi.com
6463 la costa drive # 604
boca raton florida 33433
561.367.8704
www.poundi.com

2

THE ROCK + ROLL RESCUE SQUAD
WE'RE HERE TO HELP
NAME
Rory O'Keeffe
ADDRESS
The Garage, 11a South Circular Road, Dublin 8, Ireland
CONTACT DETAILS
Telephone: + 353 1 440 4289
Mobile telephone: + 353 87 614 4043
Email: rory@therescuesquad.com
Skype: roryok
Website: www.therescuesquad.com

3

1

design firm: Crave, Inc.
art director: David Edmundson
designer: Leo Diaz
client: Pound Interactive

2

design firm: Detail Design Studio
art director: Detail Design Studio
designer: Detail Design Studio
client: Rock 'N' Roll Rescue Squad
software/hardware: Quark Xpress
paper/materials: Colorplan

3

design firm: Fresh Oil
art director: Dan Stebbings
designer: Dan Stebbings and Nelson Couto
client: Fresh Oil
software/hardware: Adobe Illustrator CS

MONICA WOOLHISER / SENIOR RECRUITER
unicru
9525 SW GEMINI DRIVE, BEAVERTON, OREGON 97008
TELE 503.596.3416 FAX 503.596.3260
EMAIL mwoolhiser@unicru.com
www.unicru.com

1

wonderboy
CHRISTINE JOHNSTON
251 Queen Street
Philadelphia, PA 19147
www.wonderboyclothing.com
info@wonderboyclothing.com
T: 215-462-1177
F: 215-462-5888

2

www.wonderboyclothing.com

3

4

1

design firm: Dotzero Design
designer: Karen Wippich and Jon Wippich
client: Unicru
software/hardware: Adobe Illustrator
paper/materials: Classic Crest

2

design firm: Johnston Duffy
art director: Martin Duffy
designer: Andy Evans
client: Wonderboy Clothing
software/hardware: Adobe Illustrator on MAC
paper/materials: 2 color and clear thermal

3

design firm: Marcus Engström
art director: Marcus Engström
designer: Marcus Engström
client: Marcus Engström
software/hardware: Adobe Illustrator
paper/materials: Matte laminate and spot UV-varnish on one side

4

design firm: Geyrhalter Design
art director: Fabian Geyrhalter
designer: Evelyn Kim
client: Inhance
software/hardware: Adobe Illustrator
paper/materials: Plastic

1

Viridian
Jean H. Green
Design Consultant
7808 South Branch
Monclova, OH 43542
419 878 0168
jean@viridiancreative.com
viridiancreative.com

2

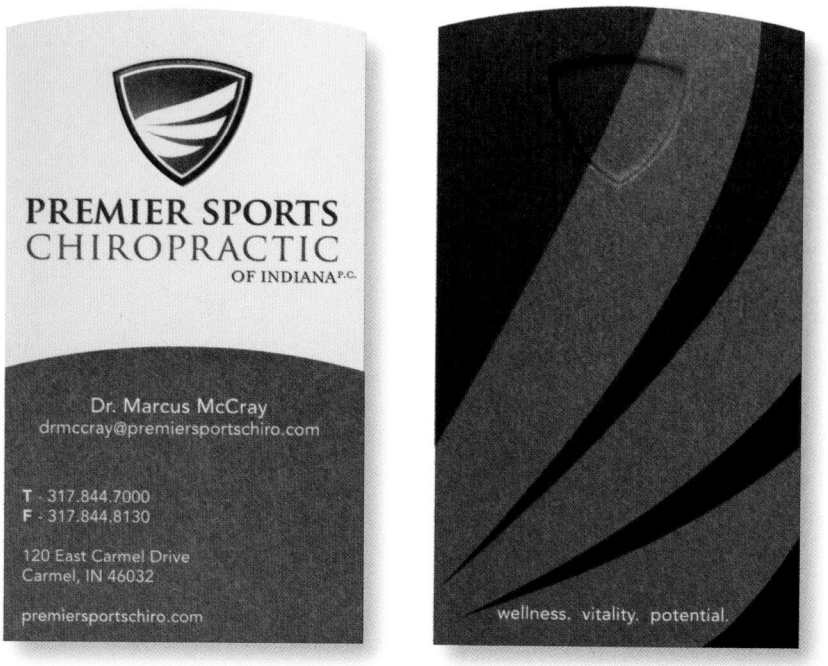
PREMIER SPORTS
CHIROPRACTIC
OF INDIANA P.C.
Dr. Marcus McCray
drmccray@premiersportschiro.com
T · 317.844.7000
F · 317.844.8130
120 East Carmel Drive
Carmel, IN 46032
premiersportschiro.com
wellness. vitality. potential.

3

4

1

design firm: Viridian
art director: Jean H. Green
client: Viridian

2

design firm: Miles Design
art director: Josh Miles
designer: Eric Folzenlogel
client: Premier Sports Chiropractic of Indiana
software/hardware: Adobe Illustrator CS2
paper/materials: 100 lb cover, offset, foil emboss

3

design firm: Funnel: Eric Kass: Utilitarian + Commercial + Fine: Art
designer: Eric Kass
client: Mike Slack
software/hardware: Adobe Illustrator CS
paper/materials: Thick uncoated paper
printing: Letterpress

4

design firm: substance151
art director: Ida Cheinman
designer: Ida Cheinman and Rick Salzman
client: LCG Technologies
software/hardware: Adobe Illustrator
paper/materials: Mohawk Navajo, 2-sided, die-cut

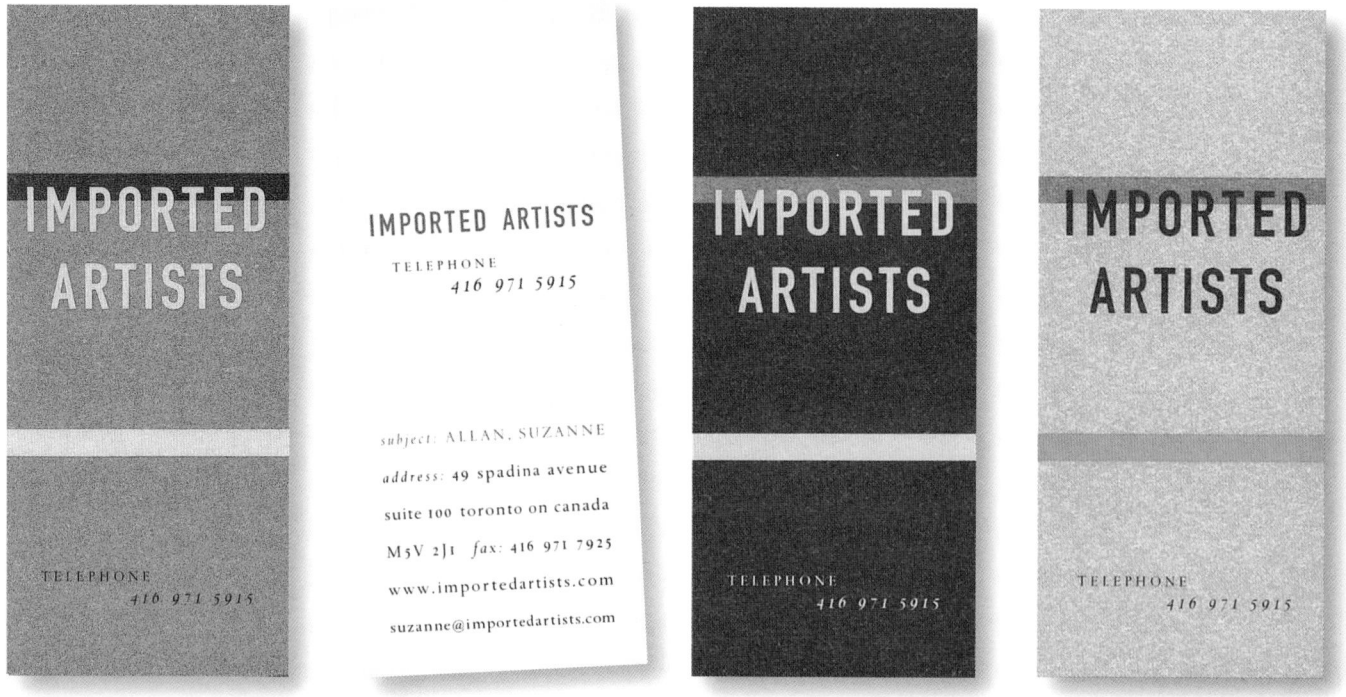
IMPORTED ARTISTS
TELEPHONE
416 971 5915
IMPORTED ARTISTS
TELEPHONE
416 971 5915
subject: ALLAN, SUZANNE
address: 49 spadina avenue
suite 100 toronto on canada
M5V 2J1 fax: 416 971 7925
www.importedartists.com
suzanne@importedartists.com
IMPORTED ARTISTS
TELEPHONE
416 971 5915
IMPORTED ARTISTS
TELEPHONE
416 971 5915

1

shannon@shannonforsell.com
DECO
RECORDS
Indianapolis Ind. United States of America
©06 Shannon Forsell
SWING'N SING'N!

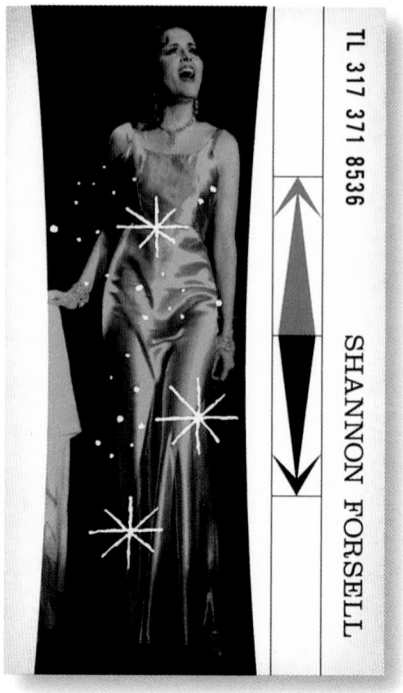
TL 317 371 8536
SHANNON FORSELL

2

3

4

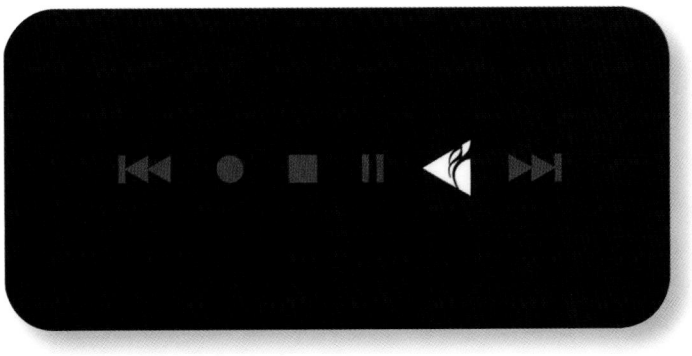

1

design firm: Blok
art director: Vanessa Eckstein
designer: Vanessa Eckstein and Frances Chen
client: Imported Artists
software/hardware: Adobe Illustrator
paper/materials: Fox River

2

design firm: Funnel: Eric Kass: Utilitarian + Commercial + Fine: Art
art director: Eric Kass
designer: Eric Kass
client: Shannon Forsell
software/hardware: Adobe Illustrator CS
paper/materials: Process offset on coated white cover with film laminate

3

design firm: 3
writer: Sam Maclay
designer: Tim McGrath
illustrator: Tim McGrath
client: Cyan Belize
software/hardware: Quark Xpress and Adobe Illustrator
paper/materials: French Paper, letterpress

4

design firm: Foda Studio
art director: Jett Butler

1

Sven Silber
Tischlermeister
Planung & Beratung | Möbelbau | Innenausbau
Türen | Restaurationen | Maßanfertigungen

Sven Silber
Tischlermeister

2

2266 Parthenais, loft 306
Montreal (Quebec) H2K 3T5
T 514.598.8181
F 514.379.5959
agence@communi-cator.com
www.communi-cator.com
IDEAS GENERATOR
COMMUNICATOR

3

Downton&Dyer Food Provider since 1878
51-53 Bourke Road Alexandria NSW 2015 Australia
T+61 2 8339 1344 F+61 2 8339 1345 M 0425 796 166
sam.choker@downtonanddyer.com.au
www.downtonanddyer.com.au
Sam Choker
Managing Director

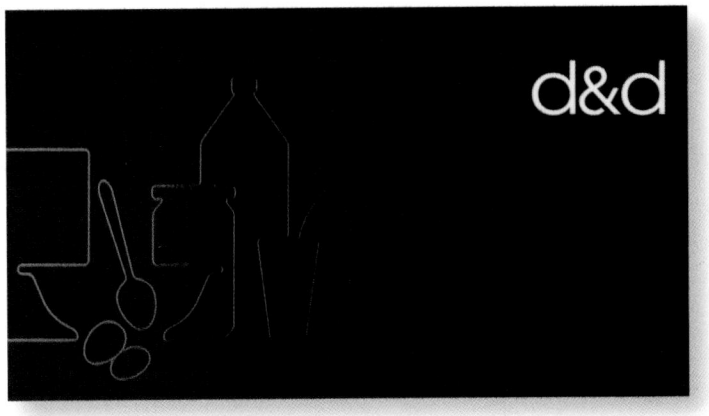
d&d

#

3
8220 La Mirada, NE, Suite 500
Albuquerque, NM 87109, USA
T: 505-293-2333 F: 505-293-1198
tmcgrath@whois3.com
(21, 63, 87, 120, 231)

3rd Edge Communications
162 Newark Avenue
Jersey City, NJ 07302, USA
T: 201-395-9960 F: 201-395-0044
3rdedge.com
(39, 128)

A

A3 Design
PO Box 43046
Charlotte, NC 28215, USA
T: 704-568-5351
Athreedesign.com
(83, 126, 139)

Ace Architects
330 2nd Street, #1
Oakland, CA 94607, USA
T: 910-452-0775 F: 910-452-1175
(68)

Adlucent
508 E 53rd Street #101
Austin, TX 78751, USA
T: 800-788-9152 F: 800-788-9152
Adlucent.com
(156)

Alphabet Arm Design
500 Harrison Avenue (3R)
Boston, MA 02218, USA
T: 617-451-9990 F: 617-451-9922
Alphabetarm.com
(23, 157)

Ana Roncha
R. Cassiano
Branco 43
Porto, 4250-084 Portugal
T: 351-93-3428805
Anaroncha.com
(41, 58)

AngryPorcupine*Design
1720 Creekside Lane
Park City, UT 84098, USA
T: 435-655-0645 F: 435-604-6970
Angryporcupine.com
(63)

Another Limited Rebellion
2701 Edgewood Avenue
Richmond, VA 23222, USA
T: 804-321-6677
Alrdesign.com
(69)

Archrival
720 O Street, Lot A
Lincoln, NE 68508, USA
T: 402-435-2525 F: 402-435-8937
Archrival.com
(49, 109)

Art Institute of Orange County
3601 W Sunflower Avenue
Santa Ana, CA 92704-9888, USA
T: 949-929-4002 F: 562-773-0794
(116)

B

Bakken Creative Co.
801 Clay Street
Oakland, CA 94607, USA
T: 507-452-8200 F: 507-452-0934
Bakkencreativeco.com
(48, 123, 207)

Base Art Co.
623 High Street
Worthington, OH 43085, USA
T: 614-841-7480 F: 614-841-7481
Baseartco.com
(30, 143)

Baseman Design Associates
221 Mather Road
Jenkintown, PA 19046, USA
T: 215-885-7157 F: 215-885-7156
Basemandesign.com
(112)

BBM&D
3 Lincoln Drive
Ventura, CA 93001, USA
T: 805-667-6671 F: 805-667-6674
Bbmd-inc.com
(19)

Belyea
1809 7th Avenue, Suite 1250
Seattle, WA 98101, USA
T: 206-682-4895 F: 206-623-8912
Belyea.com
(53)

Bennett Holzworth Design
3175 Puritan Avenue
Lincoln, NE 68502, USA
T: 402-705-9273
Bennettholzworth.com
(44, 56)

Blik
655 G Street, Suite E
San Diego, CA 92101, USA
T: 619-234-4434 F: 619-234-4494
tylerblik.com
(22)

Blok
Sombrerete 515, #7
Col. Condesa
Mexico DF, 06170, Mexico
T: 5255-5515-24-23 F: 5255-5515-24-23
Blokdesign.com
(32, 104, 118, 185, 230)

Blue Sky Design
249 Clermont Avenue
Brooklyn, NY 11205, USA
T: 718-207-4100
(37)

B.L.A. Design Company
521 South Holly Street
Columbia, SC 29205, USA
T: 803-518-4130 F: 803-781-3269
(21)

Boccalatte
PO Box 370
Surry Hills, Sydney NSW 2010
Australia
T: 61-2-9310-4309
Boccalatte.com
(74)

Boxwood Press
2 Walker Road
Kennebunk, ME 04043, USA
(93, 203)

BR
Bernstein-Rein
4600 Madison Avenue
Kansas City, MO 64112, USA
T: 816-960-5256 F: 816-960-5588
Bradv.com
(61, 139, 166, 168)

Brain Magnet
113 5th Avenue South
St Cloud, MN, USA
T: 320-257-3000 F: 320-252-7732
(218)

Brandfly
4534 Maryland Street
San Diego, CA 92116, USA
T: 619-233-0860
(158)

Briedis
8 Rolas 22-12
LV-1010, RT6A, Latvia
T: 371-2639-4647
Bairin@gmail.com
(215)

Bungalow Creative
1919 Wyandotte
Kansas City, MO 64108, USA
T: 816-421-8770 F: 816-421-8750
Bungalowcreative.com
(8, 175, 194, 195, 196)

C

Campbell Fisher Design
3333 East Camelback Road, Suite 200
Phoenix, AZ 85018, USA
T: 602-955-2707 F: 602-955-2878
Thinkcfd.com
(105, 106, 142, 187)

CDI Studios
2215a Renaissance Drive
Las Vegas, NV 89119, USA
T: 702-876-3316 F: 702-876-3317
Cdistudios.com
(214)

Chris Rooney Illustration/Design
T: 415-TCR-DRAW
Looneyrooney.com
(83)

Christiansen: Creative
511 2nd Street, #206
Hudson, WI 54016, USA
T: 715-381-8480 F: 715-381-8498
Christiansencreative.com
(38)

Cinquino + Co.
3 Garret Mountain Plaza
West Paterson, NJ 07424, USA
T: 973-523-0774 F: 973-523-0662
Cinquino.com
(88)

Color Cubic
2211 NW Front Avenue, Suite 302-E
Portland, OR 97209, USA
T: 971-832-1347
Colorcubic.com
(74)

Counterpart Communication Design
40 South Idlewild
Memphis, TN 38104, USA
T: 901-323-4900 F: 901-578-7878
Counterpartcd.com
(80)

Crave, Inc.
3100 NW Boca Raton Boulevard, Suite 109
Boca Raton, FL 33431, USA
T: 561-417-0780 F: 561-417-0490
Cravebrands.com
(49, 64, 164, 224)

Creative Spark
116 Bury New Road
Whitefield, Manchester M45 6AD,
England
T: 44-0-161-766-1331 F: 44-0-161-766-1441
Creativespark.co.uk
(135, 140, 223)

Creative Suitcase
107 Leland Street, Suite 2
Austin, TX 78704, USA
T: 512-326-3667 F: 512-326-3671
creativesuitcase.com
(187)

Creative Zumo
5030 South Liberty Street
New Orleans, LA 70115, USA
T: 504.304.9887 F: 504.895.8785
(206)

D

D4 Creative Group
161 Leverington Avenue, Suite 1001
Philadelphia, PA 19127, USA
T: 215-483-4555 F: 215-483-4554
D4creative.com
(178)

David Clark Design
1305 E 15th Street, Suite 202
Tulsa, OK 74120, USA
T: 918-295-0044 F: 918-295-0055
Davidclarkdesign.com
(62, 91, 164)

Dean Johnson Design
646 Massachusetts Avenue
Indianapolis, IN 46204, USA
T: 317-634-8020 F: 317-634-8054
Deanjohnson.com
(167)

Den Herder Design
P.O. Box 324
Central Lake, MI 49622, USA
T: 231-590-3583
(192)

Design Center, Ltd.
Knfzova 30
1000 Ljubijana, Slovenia
T: 386-1-519-5072 F: 386-1-519-5072
Cehovin.com
(138)

Design Ranch
1600 Summit
Kansas City, MO 64108, USA
T: 816-472-8668 F: 816-472-8778
Design-ranch.com
(11, 48, 66, 132, 146, 169, 204)

Design Religion
Hampton Court
Rainbow Hill
Worcester, WR3 8NF, England
T: 44-0-1905-724-707
F: 44-0-1905-724-768
Designreligion.co.uk
(97)

Detail Design Studio
11 The Friary
Bow Street
Smithfield, Dublin 7, Ireland
T: 353-1-878-3168 F: 353-1-878-3169
Detail.ie
(91, 151, 200, 224)

Di Depux
4, Eratous Street
Dafni-Athens 172-35, Greece
T: 30-210-9755850 F: 30-210-9751603
Depux.com
(34, 35, 76, 77, 109, 169, 171)

Dossier Creative, Inc.
#402-611 Alexander Street
Vancouver, BC V6A 1E1, Canada
T: 604-255-2097 F: 604-255-2097
Dossiercreative.com
(45, 67, 145)

Dot 1 Design
40 A Corporation Road
Cardiff, South Glamorgan CF11 7AW
South Wales, UK
T: 44-0-78-11-61-6123
Dot1design.co.uk
(129)

Dottie Zimmerman,
Maryville University student
7213 Balson Avenue, Apt 1F
St Louis, MO 63130, USA
T: 314-610-1562
Dottie.zimmerman@gmail.com
(33)

Dotzero Design
208 SW Stark Street, #307
Portland, OR 97204, USA
T: 503-892-9262
Dotzerodesign.com
(69, 99, 121, 184, 226)

dpd studio
408 E 1st Street, Suite 206
Long Beach, CA 90802, USA
T: 310-328-2350 F: 562-495-7101
dpdstudio.com
(107, 197)

E

Element
3292-C North High Street
Columbus, OH 43202, USA
T: 614-447-0906 F: 614-447-1417
Elementville.com
(17, 45, 84, 101, 222)

Elevator
Bana Berislavica
Split 21000, Croatia
T: 098-434-556 F: 021-332-801
Elevator.hr
(151)

Emergent Properties
Fifth Avenue Court
99 5th Avenue, Suite 249
Ottawa Ontario K1S 5P5, Canada
T: 800-521-2715 F: 800-475-2724
Emergentproperties.ca
(24)

Entermotion Design Studios
105 S Broadway
Wichita, KS 67202, USA
T: 316-264-2277 F: 316-264-2274
Entermotion.com
(17, 28, 29, 133, 144)

EPOS, Inc.
1639 16th Street
Santa Monica, CA 90404, USA
T: 310-581-2418 F: 310-581-2422
Eposinc.com
(73)

Evenson Design
4445 Overland
Culver City, CA 90230, USA
T: 310-204-1995 F: 310-204-4879
Evensondesign.com
(32, 88, 174, 203)

Eyebeam Creative LLC
1545 18th Street NW, Suite 406
Washington, D.C. 20036, USA
T: 202-518-5888 F: 202-521-1817
Eyebeamcreative.com
(181)

F

Fangman Design
107 Leland Street, Suite 2
Austin, Texas 78704, USA
T: 512-326-3676 F: 512-326-3671
Fangmandesign.com
(34, 98)

Firebelly Design
2701 W Thomas, 2nd Floor
Chicago, IL 60622, USA
T: 773-489-3200 F: 773-489-3439
Firebellydesign.com
(72)

Flipcide
3751 Robertson Boulevard
Culver City, CA 90232, USA
T: 310-559-3547, x 310 F: 310-559-9137
Flipcide.com
(115, 211)

Foda Studio
1100 W 6th, Suite B
Austin, TX 78703, USA
T: 512-615-2776 F: 512-494-0900
Fodastudio.com
(104, 165, 195, 231)

Folk Creative Ltd.
24 Luke Street
London EC2A 4NT, England
T: 44 (0) 207-739-8444
F: 44 (0) 207-033-0018
Folk.uk.com
(98)

Fresh Oil
251 Cottage Street
Pawtucket, RI 02860, USA
T: 401-709-4656 F: 401-709-4655
Freshoil.com
(225)

Frontmedia
Suite 5, Courtyard Offices
Braxted Park
Great Braxted, Essex, CM8 3GA, UK
T: 44-0-1621-890220
Frontmedia.co.uk
(94)

FSB Design
900 7.0 Andar – Itaim Bibi
São Paulo, SP 04531-003, Brazil
T: 55-11-3061-9596 F: 55-11-3086-0211
Fsb.com.br
(39)

Fuel
800 N Compton Drive, Suite 01
Hiawatha, IA 52233, USA
T: 393-319-7739 F: 393-319-7742
Fuelrefinery.com
(86, 131)

Funnel: Eric Kass:
Utilitarian + Commercial + Fine: Art
1969 Spruce Drive
Carmel, IN 46033, USA
T: 317-590-5355
Funnel.tv
(68, 229, 330)

G

Gee + Chung Design
38 Bryant Street, Suite 100
San Francisco, CA 94105, USA
T: 415-543-1192 F: 415-543-6088
Geechungdesign.com
(75)

Geyrhalter Design
2525 Main Street, Suite 205
Santa Monica, CA 90405, USA
T: 310-392-7615 x11 F: 310-396-0096
Geyrhalter.com
(181, 227)

Ginger Griffin Marketing and Design
19109 W Catawba Avenue
Cornelius, NC 28031, USA
T: 704-896-2479 F: 704-896-2517
Wehaveideas.com
(122, 148)

Greteman Group
1425 E Douglas Avenue, 2nd Floor
Wichita, KS 67211, USA
T: 316-263-1004 F: 316-263-1060
Gretemangroup.com
(27)

H

Hartford Design
954 West Washington, 4th Floor
Chicago, IL 60607, USA
T: 312-563-5600 F: 312-563-5603
Hartforddesign.com
(84)

Haute Haus Creative
107 Leland #2
Austin, TX 78704, USA
T: 512-477-7592 F: 512-326-3671
Hahacreative.com
(108, 209)

Helena Seo Design
1000 Escalon Ave, Suite 1012
Sunnyvale, CA 94085, USA
T: 408-830-0086
Helenaseo.com
(20, 52, 78, 134, 152, 183)

Home
7 Glendale Gardens
Leigh on Sea, Essex SS9 2AP
United Kingdom
T: 0044-170-271-6643
(141)

Hybrid 6 Studios
12223 Highland Avenue, Suite 220
Rancho Cucamonga, CA 91739, USA
T: 949-310-3138
Hybrid6.com
(196)

I

Idea 21
7253 Mt Sharp Road
Wimberley, TX 78676, USA
T: 512-557-4128
Jd29@txstate.edu
(176)

Imagine
The Stables
Ducie Street
Manchester M1 2JN, UK
T: +44-0-161-272-8334
imagine-cga.co.uk
(53, 70, 150)

Ingeniosus Studios, Inc.
62 W Summer Storm Circle
The Woodlands, TX 77381, USA
T: 936-718-2859
Ingstudios.com
(208)

Inovat
307 W High Street
Elizabethtown, PA, USA
T: 717-367-5446
Inovat.com
(26)

Interrobang Design Collaborative
2385 Huntington Rd
Richmond, VT 05477, USA
T: 802-434-5970 F: 802-434-6313
Interrobangdesign.com
(16)

J

James Song
489 Sanchez Street
San Francisco, CA 94114, USA
T: 415-971-0351
(189)

Jan Šabach Design
326 Degraw, #3
Brooklyn, NY 11231, USA
T: 646-220-3226
jausabach@mac.com
(200)

Jens Mogler
Germany
T: 49-7066-911318
F: 49-7066-911317
Jensmogler.de
(175)

Jill Tanenbaum Graphic Design
& Advertising Inc.
4701 Sangamore Road, Suite 235 S
Bethesda, MD 20816, USA
T: 301-229-1135, x304 F: 301-320-6620
Jtdesign.com
(154)

Joe Masquelier Designs
429 S 9th Street #17
San Jose, CA 95112, USA
T: 209-814-6951
jmasquelier@gmail.com
(172)

Joe Shouldice Design
177 Ainslie Street, Suite 3
Brooklyn, NY 11211, USA
T: 347-403-6371
Joeshouldice.com
(111)

Joel Martinez
3823 S Maryland Pkwy, #A-4
Las Vegas, NV 89119, USA
T: 702-688-3726
(206)

Johnston Duffy
803 S 4th Street, First Floor
Philadelphia, PA 19147, USA
T: 215-389-2888 F: 215-389-2889
Johnstonduffy.com
(82, 92, 186, 201, 226)

JSDS
7630 Marie Avenue
La Mesa, CA 91941, USA
T: 614-277-2585
Jsds.us
(65, 113)

Judson Design
2407 Norfolk
Houston, TX 77098, USA
T: 713-520-1096 F: 713-520-3668
Judsondesign.com
(159)

Julia Reich Design
45-50 30th Street, 7th Floor
Long Island City, NY 11101, USA
T: 718-663-8434 F: 646-224-8375
Juliareichdesign.com
(157)

Julie Grantz Design
1418 Central, Suite 31
Alameda, CA 94501, USA
T: 510-290-4579
Juliegrantz.com
(191)

Jungeschachtel
Auguststrasse 65
10117 Berlin, Germany
T: 49-178-858-2916
Jungeschachtel.de
(46)

K

KBDA
2558 Overland Avenue
Los Angeles, CA 90064, USA
T: 310-287-2400 F: 310-287-0909
Kbda.com
(155, 178)

KentLyons
Unit 203
20 Great Guildford Street,
London SE1 0HS, England
T: 20-7633-0580
Kentlyons.com
(31)

Kevin Akers Design and Imagery
4095 Lilac Ridge Road
San Ramon, CA 94582, USA
T: 925-735-1015 F: 925-735-1014
Kevinakers.com
(66, 114, 137)

Kolegram
37 St. Joseph
Gatineau, Canada
T: 819-777-5538 F: 819-777-8525
Kolegram.com
(54, 81)

L

Lance Armstrong Foundation
PO Box 161150
Austin, TX 78716, USA
T: 512-279-8381 F: 512-236-8482
Laf.org
(85)

Leanne Liew and Ken Wu
411/26 Napier Street
North Sydney 2060, Australia
T: 61-414-952-268
leanneliew@gmail.com
(102)

LeBoYe
Jl Kemang Selatan No 99 A
Jakarta Selatan 12730, Indonesia
T: 6221-7199676 F: 6221-7199677
Leboyedesign.com
(86)

Lefty Lexington Design
217 W Main Street, #2
Stoughton, WI 53589, USA
T: 608-205-2067
Leftylexington.com
(202)

Lemley Design
2727 Fairview Avenue East, Suite F
Seattle, WA 98102, USA
T: 206-285-6900 x 202 F: 206-285-6906
Lemleydesign.com
(55)

Limb Design
7026 Old Katy Road
Houston, TX 77024, USA
T: 713-529-1117 F: 713-529-1558
Limbdesign.com
(24, 136, 186)

Liquid Agency
448 S Market Street
San Jose, CA 95113, USA
T: 408-850-8800 F: 408-850-8825
Liquidagency.com
(70, 180)

Liska + Associates
515 N State Street, 23rd Floor
Chicago, IL 60610, USA
T: 312-644-4400 F: 312-644-9560
Liska.com
(81, 212, 217)

Lizette Gecel
4706 Augusta Avenue
Richmond, VA 23230, USA
T: 804-359-1711
Lizettegecel2@verizon.net
(174)

Lloyds Graphic Design Ltd.
17 Westhaven Place
Blenheim, 7201, New Zealand
T: 643-578-6955 F: 643-578-6955
lloydgraphics@xtra.co.uk
(135)

Lolight Design
2107 Malvern Hills Drive
Austin, TX 78745, USA
T: 512-587-7690 F: 866-494-8194
Lolight.com
(79, 136, 201)

Lotta Odelius
Ord Bild Form
Parkgatan 6
11230 Stockholm, Sweden
T: 46-709-1999-93 F: 46-8-445-87-99
Lottaodelius.se
(25)

Louviere + Vanessa
732 Mazant Street
New Orleans, LA 70117, USA
T: 504-296-5467
Louviereandvanessa,com
(14, 126)

M

Marcus Engström
Svartmangatan 9
11129 Stockholm, Sweden
T: 46-704-2465-13 F: 46-8-445-87-99
Marcusengstrom.com
(227)

Markcom Consulting Group
1327 Coronado Terrace
Los Angeles, CA 90026, USA
T: 213-483-1416 F: 213-596-1437
Markcomgroup.com
(191)

Matthew Schwartz Design Studio
611 Broadway, Suite 430
New York, NY 10012, USA
T: 212-925-6460 F: 212-260-7951
Ms-ds.com
(118, 179)

Mayda Freije Makdessi
P.O. Box 165249, Ashrafieh, Sassine Street
Beirut, Lebanon
T: 961-70-987659 F: 961-1-444232
Lyenno@inco.com.lb
(188)

MBA
Austin, Texas
T: 512-971-7820
www.your-mba.com
(23, 29, 130, 160, 198, 205, 216)

MDG
13 Water Street, Third Floor
Holliston, MA 01746, USA
T: 508-429-0755 F: 508-429-0766
M-d-g.com
(87)

Meagan Goldberg
5400 W Parmer Lane #712
Austin, TX 78727, USA
T: 512-771-5430 F: 512-331-7321
Meagangoldberg.com
(43)

Miles Design
5170 East 65th Street
Indianapolis, IN 46220, USA
T: 317-915-8693 F: 317-915-1103
milesdesign.com
(26, 38, 59, 96, 99, 148, 176, 216, 228)

MINE™
190 Putnam Street
San Francisco, CA 94110, USA
T: 415-647-6463 F: 415-647-6468
Minesf.com
(35, 51, 70, 89, 100)

Mingovits Design
101 W 23rd Street, #2176
New York, NY 10011, USA
T: 212-683-0003
Mingovits@earthlink.net
(125)

Miriello Grafico
419 West G Street
San Diego, CA 92101, USA
T: 619-234-1124 F: 619-234-1960
Miriellografico.com
(22, 153)

Murillo Design, Inc.
6247 John Chapman
San Antonio, TX 78240, USA
T: 210-215-8789
Murillodesign.com
(95, 134, 177)

N

Nassar Design
11 Park Street, Suite 1
Brookline, MA 02446, USA
T: 617-264-2862 F: 617-264-2861
n.nassar@verizon.net
(119)

Nicole Nicolaus
c/o Auour Eyjolfsdottir, Dalhus 78
112 Reykjavik, Iceland
T: 00354-661-2620
Augenspagat.com
(189)

Nocturnal Graphic Design Studio
5455 East Ron Rico Road
Cave Creek, AZ 85331, USA
T: 480-688-4207
Nocturnaldesign.com
(9)

Nothing: Something: NY
242 Wythe Avenue, Studio #3
Brooklyn, NY 11211, USA
T: 646-221-9972 F: 718-388-7840
Nothingsomething.com
(25, 93, 115, 193)

O

Onemethod Inc.
7145 West Credit Avenue
Building 1, Suite 102
Mississauga, Ontario L5N 6J7, Canada
T: 905-603-0180 F: 905-603-8180
Onemethod.com
(100)

Orangeseed Design
800 Washington Avenue N #461
Minneapolis, MN 55401, USA
T: 612-252-9757 F: 612-252-9760
Orangeseed.com
(131)

Origami
1452 Rue Saint Mathieu
Montréal, Quebec H3H 2H9, Canada
T: 514-933-1222 F: 514-933-1645
Origami.qc.ca
(18)

Originalia: A Design Studio
1641 Mears Avenue
Cincinnati, OH 45230, USA
T: 513-310-3527 F: 859-572-6512
Originalia.org
(36)

P

P22
PO Box 770
Buffalo, NY 14213, USA
T: 716-885-4470 F: 716-885-4482
P22.com
(64)

Pagliuco Design Company
213 W Institute Place, Suite 508
Chicago, IL 60610, USA
T: 312-943-4281 F: 312-943-6946
Pagliuco.com
(40, 79, 188, 208)

Paper Tower Studios
626 Congdon Avenue
Elgin, IL 60120, USA
T: 847-513-2063 F: 866-651-8364
Papertowerstudios.com
(222)

Paragon Marketing Communications
Salmiya, Salem Al-Mubarak Street
Al-Fanar Mall, 1st Floor, Office 21J
P.O. Box 6097 Salmiya 22071, Kuwait
T: 965-5716063-5716068-5716039
F: 965-5715985
Paragonmc.com
(13, 213)

Philadelphia University Design
221 Mather Road
Jenkintown, MA 19046, USA
T: 215-885-7157 F: 215-885-7156
Basemandesign.com
(15)

Philippe Archontakis
5685 6th Avenue
Montréal, Québec H1Y 2R1, Canada
T: 514-909-3122
Philippearchontakis.com
(217, 218, 233)

Pinpoint Communications
426 South Military Trail
Deerfield Beach, FL 33442, USA
T: 954-574-0601 F: 954-574-0609
Pinpoint-comm.com
(111, 209)

Popcorn Initiative
1602 Robin Road
Orlando, FL 32803, USA
T: 407-228-6601 F: 407-228-9803
Popcorninitiative.com
(19)

Pressure
2820 14th Avenue, Suite 101
Markham, ON L3R 0S9, Canada
T: 905-305-0979 F: 905-305-0415
Pressure.org
(10)

R

R975
Emanuel-Geibel-Strasse 6
Wiesbaden 65185, Germany
T: 49-611-42-2437
R975.de
(95, 223)

Rager 1
55 E 10th Avenue
Montreal, Quebec H1Y 2R1, Canada
T: 604-738-7696
Rager1.com
(154)

Reactor
3111 Wyandotte, Suite 204
Kansas City, MO 64111, USA
T: 816-841-4929
Yourreactor.com
(37, 156, 199)

Red Circle Agency
251 1st Avenue N, Suite 400
Minneapolis, MN 55401, USA
T: 612-372-4612 F: 612-372-4617
Redcircleagency.com
(50, 161)

Ritzy Periwinkle
849 Parkman Avenue #2
Los Angeles, CA 90026, USA
T: 323-230-9600 F: 323-230-9600
Ritzyperiwinkle.com
(179)

Rome & Gold Creative
1606 Central SE, Suite 102
Albuquerque, NM 87106, USA
T: 505-897-0870 F: 505-843-7500
Rgcreative.com
(124, 127)

Root Idea
Room 208, Catil Bldg
44 Tsun Yip St
Kwan Tong, KLN BS2, Hong Kong
T: 852-2973-0056 F: 852-2973-0035
Rootidea.com
(13, 106)

Rusty George Creative
732 Broadway, Suite 302
Tacoma, WA 98402, USA
T: 253-284-2140 F: 253-284-2142
Rustygeorge.com
(94)

S

Sagmeister Inc.
222 W 14th Street
New York, NY 10011, USA
T: 212-647-1789 F: 212-647-1788
Sagmeister.com
(220)

Salterbaxter
202 Kensington Church Street
London W8 4DP, UK
T: 44-20-7229-5720
F: 44-20-7229-5721
Salterbaxter.com
(90)

Sandy Gin Design
1220 Oak Street
San Carlos, CA 94070, USA
T: 650-591-2418 F: 650-591-2418
designsg@earthlink.net
(121)

Scott Adams Design Associates
2266 East Main Street, Suite A
Columbus, OH 43209, USA
T: 614-404-4308 F: 614-239-8390
Sadesigna.com
(105)

Seltzer
45 Newbury Street #406
Boston, MA 02116, USA
T: 617-353-0303 F: 617-262-0255
Seltzerdesign.com
(55)

Sheriff Design
7943 Park Avenue
Elkins Park, PA 19027, USA
T: 215-782-9185 F: 215-782-9186
Sheriff@voicenet.com
(149, 214)

Sherry Matthews
200 S Congress
Austin, TX 78704, USA
T: 512-478-4397 F: 512-478-2892
Sherrymatthews.com
(170)

Shine Advertising
612 West Main Street, #105
Madison, WI 53703, USA
T: 608-442-7373 F: 608-442-7374
Shinenorth.com
(16, 103, 144)

Shoehorn
1010 E 11th Street
Austin, TX 78703, USA
T: 512-478-4190 F: 512-477-5104
Shoehorndesign.com
(133)

Sibley Peteet Design–Austin
522 E 6th Street
Austin, TX 78701, USA
T: 512-473-2333
Spdaustin.com
(103, 182, 190)

Sibley Peteet Design–Dallas
3232 McKinney Avenue, Suite 1200
Dallas, TX 75204, USA
T: 214-969-1050 F: 214-969-7585
Spddallas.com
(33, 108)

SKA
Rua Fernão Vaz
Dourado 62
4150-322 Porto Portugal
T: 351-226-165-569 F: 351-226-165-570
Ska.pt
(60)

SK+G Advertising
8912 Spanish Ridge Avenue
Las Vegas, NV 89148, USA
T: 702-478-4060 F: 702-478-4360
Skgadv.com
(14, 52)

smashLAB
405-318 Homer Street
Vancouver, BC V6B 2V2, Canada
T: 604-683-2250 F: 866-829-6128
Smashlab.com
(51, 119, 150, 183, 213)

Sommese Design
100 Rose Drive
Port Matilda, PA 16870, USA
T: 814-353-1951 F: 814-863-8706
lannys@psu.edu
(12)

Sparc, Inc.
824 Humboldt
Winnetka, IL 60093, USA
T: 847-784-3100 F: 847-784-3101
richardcassis@hotmail.com
(15)

Steinzeit-mediendesign
Ottwellerstrasse 26a
40476 Düsseldorf, Germany
T: 49-211-48-46-84-27
F: 49-211-48-46-84-26
Steinzeit-mediendesign.de
(219, 232)

Subplot Design, Inc.
301-308 Homer Street
Vancouver, BC V6B 2V2, Canada
T: 604-685-2990 F: 604-685-2909
Subplot.com
(75, 114, 210)

substance151
2304 E Baltimore Street
Baltimore, MD 21224, USA
T: 410-732-8379 F: 425-940-7800
Substance151.com
(160, 198, 229)

Substância 4 Comunicação e Design
Rua Almirante Tamandare, 66-sala 1215-Flamengo
Rio de Janeiro, RJ 22210-060, Brazil
T: 55-21-3507-3452 F: 55-21-3507-3452
Substancia4.com.br
(43)

Swirl
808 N Alamo
San Antonio, TX 78215, USA
T: 210-226-6822 F: 877-820-1397
Getswirled.com
(210)

Switch Creative
575 S Homles
Memphis, TN 38111, USA
T: 901-230-0888 F: 901-320-1622
Switchcreative.com
(58, 82, 126)

T

The Decoder Ring Design Concern
410 Congress, Suite 200
Austin, TX 78701, USA
T: 512-236-1610 F: 512-597-1848
Thedecoderring.com
(158, 168, 192, 203, 204)

The Design Firm
1 Vancouver Avenue
Toronto, ON M4L 2S7, Canada
T: 416-995-0243
Thedesignfirm.ca
(145)

The Human Race
858 Meigs Street, #5
Rochester, NY 14620, USA
T: 607-342-2269
Ehtnax@yahoo.com
(92)

The Matchbox Studio
3900 Elm Street
Dallas, TX 75226, USA
T: 214-939-3100 F: 214-939-3400
Matchboxstudio.com
(31, 112)

There
Level 1, 16 Foster Street
Surry Hills, Sydney NSW 2010, Australia
T: 02-9280-1477 F: 02-9280-1499
There.com.au
(12, 113, 233)

Thielen Designs
115 Gold Avenue SW, Suite 209
Albuquerque, NM 87102, USA
T: 505-205-3157
Thielendesign.com
(85)

Think Studio, NYC
234 West 16th Street
New York, NY 10011, USA
T: 646-415-8325
Thinkstudionyc.com
(67, 142)

Timber Design Co.
4402 N College Avenue
Indianapolis, IN 46205, USA
T: 317-213-8509 F: 317-921-0948
Timberdesignco.com
(20, 185)

Trade Creative Services
1050 Techwood Drive
Atlanta, GA 30318, USA
T: 404-575-7191 F: 404-885-0111
Turner.com
(110)

Turnstyle
2219 NW Market Street
Seattle, WA 98107, USA
T: 206-297-7350 F: 206-297-7390
Turnstylestudio.com
(41, 73, 101, 122, 133, 137, 165)

Typesync Studio
10 Mountain Avenue, #B
Norwood, WA 02062, USA
T: 617-953-8211
Typesync.com
(28)

U

Ultra Design
Rua Padre Anchieta 2454
Conjunto 503, Curitiba 80730 000, Brasil
T: 55-41-3016-3023 F: 55-41-3016-3023
Ultradesign.com.br
(54)

V

Viridian
7808 South Branch
Monclova, OH 43542, USA
T: 419-878-0168
Viridiancreative.com
(228)

Vyant Group
810 Lawrence Drive, Suite 220
Thousand Oaks, CA 91320, USA
T: 805-214-0999 F: 805-214-0997
Vyantgroup.com
(166)

W

W Design
2922 Whidden
Boise, ID 83702, USA
T: 208-345-9562
Wdesignboise.com
(11)

Willoughby Design Group
602 Westport Road
Kansas City, MO 64111, USA
T: 816-561-4189 F: 816-561-5052
Willoughbydesign.com
(27, 42, 141, 152, 155)

Wing Chan Design, Inc.
167 Perry Street, Suite 5C
New York, NY 10014, USA
T: 212-727-9109 F: 212-727-8742
Wingchandesign.com
(9)

WOW Branding
101-1300 Richards Street
Vancouver, BC V6B 3G6, Canada
T: 604-368-5655
Wowbranding.com
(125)

Wyld Stallions
4-04 Clerkenwell Close
London EC1 R0AT, UK
T: 44-0-207-014-3830
(71)

Y

YOUN Graphic and Interactive Design
7589 Mallard Drive
Mobile, AL 36695, USA
T: 251-461-1437 F: 251-414-8194
Kwyoun@hotmail.com
(128)

Z

Zande + Newman Design
902 Jefferson Avenue, No 1
New Orleans, LA 70115, USA
T: 504-891-4526 F: 504-891-3919
Zandenewman.com
(62, 78, 96, 162, 212)

Zócalo Design
2401 E Sixth Street, #3034
Austin, TX 78702, USA
T: 512-851-1887 F: 512-851-1887
Zocalodesign.com
(158)

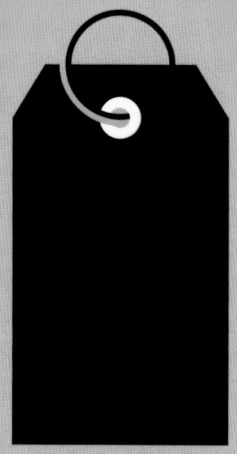

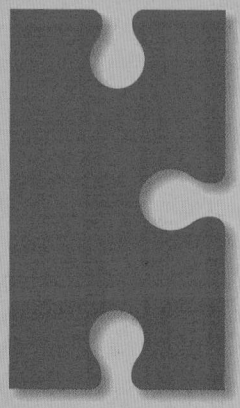

ABOUT THE AUTHOR

Rex Peteet is founding partner and principal designer of Sibley/Peteet, in Austin, Texas. The firm specializes in corporate communications and comprehensive design strategies for clients such as the Sid Richardson Museum, Tivoli/IBM, AMD, GSD&M, Temple-Inland, Haggar Apparel, Mary Kay Cosmetics,Farah/Savane, Milton Bradley (including Scattergories andGuesstures), Dave & Buster's, Brinker International (including Romano's Macaroni Grill and Chili's), Mr. Gatti's Pizza, and Fuddruckers.

Peteet has won numerous regional and national design awards including the New York Art Directors Show, the Los Angeles Art Directors Show, and AR100 and has had several works selected for the permanent collection of the Library of Congress. He has been widely published and featured in many industry magazines and annuals including *Communication Arts*, *Print*, *AIGA*, *Graphis*, *Step*, and *HOW*. In 2005, Peteet was the recipient of the Dallas Society of Visual Communications' highest honor and career achievement award, The Golden Egg. Peteet is also a founding member of the first Texas chapter of AIGA and currently sits on the Advisory Board of AIGA Austin.